COURAGE

Legends and Role Models

Emerson Klees

Emerson Klees

Cameo Press, Rochester, New York

Cameo Press
P. O. Box 18131
Rochester, New York 14618

Library of Congress Control Number 2017905929

ISBN 978-1-891046-27-8

Printed in the United States of America
9 8 7 6 5 4 3 2 1

DEDICATION

This book is dedicated to Reverend Jim Lawlor, a down-to-earth person with a good sense of humor. His sermons are based partly on the Gospel and partly on the society of today. He is a person we would do well to emulate.

OTHER BOOKS BY EMERSON KLEES

Role Models of Human Values Series

*One Plus One Equals Three—Pairing Man / Woman Strengths:
    Role Models of Teamwork*
*Entrepreneurs In History—Success vs. Failure: Entrepreneurial
    Role Models*
Staying With It: Role Models of Perseverance
The Drive to Succeed: Role Models of Motivation
The Will to Stay With It: Role Models of Determination
Emotional Intelligence: People Smart Role Models
Emotional Intelligence: People Smart Role Models II
Emotional Intelligence: People Smart Role Models III
Rebounding from Setbacks: Role Models of Resilience
The Creators: Role Models of Creativity
Success: Role Models of Winners

The Moral Navigator: Stories From Around the World
Inspiring Legends and Tales With a Moral I
Inspiring Legends and Tales With a Moral II
Inspiring Legends and Tales With a Moral III

Books About New York State and the Finger Lakes Region

People of the Finger Lakes Region
Legends and Stories of the Finger Lakes Region
The Erie Canal in the Finger Lakes Region
Underground Railroad Tales With Routes Through the Finger Lakes
More Legends and Stories of the Finger Lakes Region
The Women's Rights Movement and the Finger Lakes Region
The Crucible of Ferment: New York's "Psychic Highway"
The Iroquois Confederacy: History and Legends
Rochester Lives
Wineries of the Finger Lakes Region—100 Wineries
Persons, Places, and Things of the Finger Lakes Region
A Song of the Vine: A Reflection on Life
Paul Garrett: Dean of American Winemakers
Finger Lakes Wineries: A Pictorial History

THE ROLE MODELS OF HUMAN VALUES SERIES

"Example teaches better than precept. It is the best modeler of the character of men and women. To set a lofty example is the richest bequest a man [or woman] can leave behind."

Samuel Smiles

The Role Models of Human Values Series provides examples of role models and of lives worthy of emulation. The human values depicted in this series include perseverance, motivation, determination, resilience, creativity, and courage. Role models are presented in biographical sketches of historical figures that describe the environment within which they strived and delineate their personal characteristics.

These profiles illustrate how specific human values helped achievers reach their goals in life. We can learn from these examples in strengthening the human values that are so important to our success and happiness. The Introduction in each book highlights the factors that contributed to these achievers' success.

PREFACE

"Success is not final. Failure is not fatal. It is the courage to continue that counts."

Winston Churchill

This book provides ten ancient and moral legends about courage and fifteen role models of individuals who were courageous. Biographical sketches for the role models represent six areas of endeavor. These individuals displayed other strong personal characteristics, including perseverance, motivation, determination, resilience, and creativity, as discussed in other books in the Human Values Series. These individuals had multiple strong human qualities. They provide us with examples of behavior to emulate. We can learn from these individuals to be more courageous in our own lives.

Ancient Legends

Moral Legends

Luminaries and and Notables

Achievers and Activists

Victors and Leaders

TABLE OF CONTENTS

Page No.

INTRODUCTION

"I learned that courage was not the absence of fear, but the triumph over it. The brave man is not he who does not feel afraid, but he who conquers that fear."

Nelson Mandela

Courage is our willingness to deal with anxiety and fear. Physical courage is to confront immediate danger, pain, threat of death, or death. Moral courage includes acting ethically when confronted with opposing views, potential scandal, or shame.

In *Courage: The Politics of Life and Limb,* Richard Avramenko observed:

> Man is nothing other than what he makes of himself, and nothing is more difficult than to make a courageous man . . . If there were nothing to fear in the world, there would be no need to make courageous men and women of ourselves. Without conflict, the difficult task of making ourselves courageous can be replaced with whatever we want to make of ourselves.

Anxiety is a state of mind that is not prepared to deal with perceived negative events. It is perceived as a condition leading to avoiding a threat (known as the fight-or-flight response). Anxiety is related to fear, which is an emotional response to becoming aware of threat.

Fear tends to be short-lived, focused on the present, concerned with a particular threat, sometimes leading to fleeing the scene. Anxiety is considered long acting, focused on the future and concerned with a broader threat, motivating an individual to become cautious.

In *Why Courage Matters,* John McCain provided a number of outstanding profiles of heroes, many of whom are military heroes. However, one does not have to be in battle to be a hero,

9

He noted:

> If you do things you think you cannot do, you'll find your resistance, your hope, your dignity, and your courage grow stronger every time you prove it. You will someday face harder choices that may very well require more courage. You're getting ready for them. You're getting ready to have courage, and when these moments come, unbidden but certain, and you choose well, your courage will be recognized by those who matter most to you.

It is easy to agree with the observation of Winston Churchill: "Courage is the first of human qualities . . . because it guarantees all others."

CHAPTER 1

ANCIENT LEGENDS

"The charm of the best courages is that they are inventions, inspirations, flashes of genius."

Ralph Waldo Emerson, *Society and Solitude: Courage*

Courage

The Brave Three Hundred

The famous battle of Thermopylae, a Greek pass leading into Thessaly, was fought in 480 BC. King Xerxes of Persia led his army into Greece along the coast between Mount Oeta and the Maliac Gulf. The only route into Greece from the east was through the narrow pass at Thermopylae, named for hot springs nearby.

The pass was guarded by Leonidas, king of the Spartans, with only a few thousand men. They were greatly outnumbered by the Persian army. Leonidas positioned his warriors in the narrowest part of the pass, where a few men armed with long spears could hold off an entire company. The Persian attack began at dawn.

Arrows rained down on the Greek defenders, but their shields deflected them, and their long spears held back the Persians. The invaders attacked again and again with terrible losses. Finally Xerxes sent his best troops, known as the Ten Thousand Immortals, into battle but they fared no better against the determined Greeks.

After two days of fighting, Leonidas still held the pass. That night a Greek who knew the local terrain well was brought into Xerxes's camp. He told Xerxes that the pass was not the only way through. A hunter's footpath wound the long way around, to a trail along the spine of the mountain. It was held by a handful of Greeks who could easily be overcome, and then the Spartan army could be attacked from the rear. The treacherous plan worked, but a few Greeks escaped to warn Leonidas.

The Greeks knew that if they did not abandon the pass at once, they would be trapped. However, Leonidas also realized that he must delay Xerxes longer while the Greeks prepared the defenses of their cities. He made the difficult decision to order most of his troops to slip through the mountains and back to their cities, where they would be needed. He retained three hundred of his Spartans and a small number of Thespians and Thebans and prepared to defend the pass until the end.

Xerxes and his army advanced. The Spartans stood fast, but one by one they fell. When their spears broke, they fought with swords and daggers. All day they kept the Persian army at bay. By sundown, not one Spartan was left alive.

Xerxes had taken the pass, but at a cost of thousands of men and a delay of several days. This delay was critical. The Greeks

12

were able to gather their forces, including their navy, and soon drove the Persians back to Asia. Many years later, a monument was erected at the pass of Thermopylae in memory of the courageous stand of a few in the defense of their homeland.

Moral: The courage of the few can save the many.

Based on: James Baldwin, "The Brave Three Hundred," *Favorite Tales of Long Ago*

David and Goliath

Jesse, who lived long ago in Bethlehem, had eight strong, resolute sons. His youngest son was David. As a boy, David was strong and healthy with a pleasing appearance. When his older brothers drove the sheep to the fields, he went with them. David loved the outdoors and ran around the hillsides listening to the rippling water in the brooks and the songs of birds perched in the trees. He made up songs about the beautiful things that he saw and heard. He was happy and grew in strength.

David did not lack courage. His eyes were sharp and his aim was sure. When he placed a stone in his sling, he never missed his target. As he grew older, he was given the responsibility of tending part of the flock of sheep. One day as he watched his sheep from the hillside, a lion dashed out of the nearby woods and seized a lamb. David leaped to his feet and ran toward the lion without hesitating.

David had no fear; he just wanted to save the lamb that he was responsible for. He jumped on the lion, seized his head, and, with his wooden staff as his only weapon, slew him. Another day, a bear came out of the woods and approached the flock. David killed the bear also.

Soon after these events, the Philistines assembled an army and marched over the hills to drive the people of Israel from their homes. King Saul marshaled the Israelite army and went out to meet his enemies. David's three oldest brothers joined King Saul's army, but David was left at home to tend the sheep. His brothers told him that he was too young to fight; besides, someone had to protect the flocks.

Forty days passed and no word was received from King Saul's army. Jesse asked David to go to the encampment to take food to his brothers and see how they were doing. David traveled to the hill on which King Saul's army was camped. He heard much shouting and saw that the armies were formed to do battle. David walked through the ranks and finally found his brothers. As he stood talking with them, the shouting stopped, and the armies became very quiet.

David saw that a giant stood on the opposite hillside. As the giant paced up and down, his armor glistened in the sun. His sword and shield were so heavy that none of King Saul's men could have lifted them. David's brothers said that this was the great giant, Goliath. Every day, he walked towards them and called out challenges to the men of Israel. No one in the Israelite army dared to take him on.

David was astounded; he wondered if the men of Israel were afraid. He asked how they could let this Philistine defy the army of Israel. Was no one willing to go out and meet him? Eliab, David's oldest brother, grew angry and accused his brother of being haughty and proud. He jeered that David had come merely to watch a battle, and that he should be at home tending the sheep. David told Eliab that the keeper was tending the sheep, and that their father had asked him to come. He added that he was glad that he had come, because he was going to take on the giant.

David said that he had no fear of the giant because the God of Israel was with him. Some men standing nearby told King Saul of David's willingness to fight Goliath. King Saul asked them to bring David to him. When the king saw how young David was, he tried to discourage him. David told King Saul how he had killed the lion and the bear with his bare hands and a staff. David said that the good Lord had delivered him from them and would also deliver him from the hands of this oversized Philistine.

King Saul told David to undertake his task and prayed that the Lord would go with him. The king offered David the use of his sword, coat of mail, and helmet. David refused them, admitting that he was not skilled in their use. He knew that a man must win his battles on his own terms and with his own weapons.

David left the encampment with just his staff, his shepherd's bag, and his sling. He ran down to the brook at the foot of the hill. He leaned down and picked up five smooth stones from the brook and dropped them into his bag. The great giant stalked toward David while the men of both armies looked on in awe from the hillsides.

When the giant saw saw how young David was, he was angry. He thought the men of Israel were mocking him by sending one so young against him. Goliath asked if the youth considered him a dog to be attacked by sticks. He told David to turn back or he would feed his flesh to the beasts of the field and the birds of the air. Then the giant cursed David in the name of all of his gods.

15

David was still without fear. He called out that Goliath came to fight with a sword, a spear, and a shield, but that he came in the name of the Lord, the God of the army of Israel, whom the Philistines had defied. He told the giant that the Lord would deliver him into his hands and defeat him, and all would know about the God of Israel.

The giant ran toward David, and David advanced even faster toward the giant. David reached into his bag for a stone and loaded it into his sling. His keen eye found the place in the Giant's forehead where the helmet joined. He drew his sling, and, with all the force of his strong right arm, hurled the stone. The stone whizzed through the air and struck deep into the vulnerable place in Goliath's forehead. His huge body tottered and then toppled to the ground. As Goliath lay with his face toward the ground, David ran quickly to his side, drew the giant's sword, and severed his head from his body.

When the army of Israel saw this, they shouted and ran down the hillside toward the Philistine army. As the Philistines realized that their greatest warrior had been slain by a young man, they fled, leaving their tents and all their belongings as spoils for the men of Israel.

At the conclusion of the battle, King Saul asked for the young victor to be brought before him. He asked David to stay with him as his own son instead of returning to Jesse's house. David stayed with King Saul and eventually was given command of the army of Israel. All Israel honored him. Years later, when Saul stepped down as king, David succeeded him.

Moral: Courage can overcome what appear to be unsurmountable odds.

Based on: J. Berg Esenwein and Marietta Stockard, "David and Goliath," *Children's Stories and How to Tell Them*

St. George and the Dragon

Centuries ago, when chivalry was still alive, one brave knight who distinguished himself was Sir George. He was so good, kind, and noble that people called him St. George. No robbers threatened people who lived near his castle; they knew that St. George would protect them. Wild animals were either killed or driven away so children could play in nearby woods without fear.

One day St. George traveled around the countryside and saw men busy at work in the fields, women singing at work in their homes, and children cheerfully at play. He noted that the people were all safe and happy. He concluded that they didn't need him anymore. He thought, "But somewhere perhaps there is trouble and fear. There may be someplace where little children cannot play in safety. A woman may have been carried away from her home, or perhaps there are even dragons left to be slain. Tomorrow I shall ride away and never stop until I find work that only a knight can do."

Early the next morning, St. George put on his shining armor and helmet and fastened his sword to his belt. Then he mounted his great white horse and rode out of his castle gate down the steep, rough road. He sat straight and looked brave and strong, as one would expect of a noble knight. He rode through the village and into the countryside where he saw rich fields filled with grain; peace and plenty were everywhere.

St. George rode on until he came to a part of the country that he had never seen before. No one was working in the fields, and the houses he passed were empty and silent. A wheatfield had been trampled and burned, and the grass along the road had been scorched. St. George drew up his horse and look around the countryside. Desolation and silence were everywhere. He asked himself, "What can be the dreadful thing that has driven people from their homes?" He was determined to find out and to help them if he could.

Unfortunately, there was no one around to ask, so St. George rode on until he saw the walls of a city. He was sure that he would find someone who could tell him the cause of the desolation, so he spurred his horse. As he approached the city walls, the great gate opened, and he saw crowds gathered inside the walls. Some people were weeping, and all of them seemed afraid.

As St. George watched, he saw a beautiful young woman dressed in white, with a scarlet girdle around her waist, walk through the gate by herself. The gate was closed and locked after her; she walked down the road, weeping. She did not see St. George, who rode over to her. When he reached her side, he asked why she was crying. She said, "Oh, Sir Knight, ride quickly from this place. You do not know the danger you are in."

St. George said, "Danger! Do you think a knight would flee from danger? Besides, you, a fair girl, are here alone. Do you think a knight would leave you so? Tell me your trouble so that I may help you."

She cried out, "No! No! Hurry away. You would only lose your life. A terrible dragon is nearby. He may come out at any moment. One breath of fire would destroy you if he found you here. Go! Go quickly!"

St. George said, "Tell me more. Why are you here alone to meet this dragon? Are there no men left in the city?"

The maiden said, "My father, the king, is old and feeble. He has only me to help him take care of his people. This terrible dragon has driven them from their homes, carried away their cattle, and ruined their crops. They have all come within the walls for their safety. For weeks now, the dragon has come to the very gates of the city. We have been forced to give him two sheep every day for his breakfast.

"Yesterday there were no more sheep left to give. The dragon demanded that unless a young maiden were given to him today, he would break down the walls and destroy the city. The people cried to my father to save them, but he could do nothing. I am going to give myself to the dragon. Perhaps if he has me, he may spare our people."

St. George said, "Lead the way, brave princess. Show me where this monster may be found." When the princess saw St. George's flashing eyes and strong right arm as he drew his sword, she was no longer afraid. Turning, she led the way to a shining pool. She whispered, "That's where he stays. See the water move. He is waking up."

St. George saw the head of the dragon emerge from the surface of the water. He crawled out of the pool. When he saw St. George, he roared in rage and plunged toward him. Smoke and flames flew from his nostrils, and he opened his great jaws as though he were about to swallow both knight and horse.

St. George yelled, waved his sword over his head, and rode at the dragon. The blows from St. George's sword came rapidly and furiously. It was a terrible battle. Finally, the dragon was wounded. He howled with pain and plunged at St. George, opening his mouth close to the brave knight's head. St. George aimed carefully and then struck with all of his might straight down the throat of the dragon, who fell dead at his horse's feet.

St. George shouted for joy at his victory. He called the princess, who came and stood beside him. He asked her for the girdle around her waist, which he wound around the dragon's neck. He used it to pull the dragon back to the city so the people could see that it would never harm them again.

When they saw that St. George had brought the Princess back safely and had slain the dragon, people threw open the gates of the city and shouted with joy. The king came out of the palace to see why they were shouting. When he saw that his daughter was safe, he was the happiest of all. The king said, "Oh brave knight, I am old and weak. Stay here and help me guard my people from harm."

St. George agreed to stay for as long as he was needed. He lived in the palace and helped the old king take care of his people. When the old king died, St. George was made his successor. The people were happy and safe as long as they had such a brave and good man for their king.

Moral: The strong should come to the aid of the weak.

Based on: J. Berg Esenwein and Marietta Stockard,
          "St. George and the Dragon," *Children's Stories and How to Tell Them*

Horatius at the Bridge

At the end of the sixth century BC, the Roman people were at war with the Etruscans, who lived on the other side of the Tiber River from Rome. The Etruscan king, Lars Porsena, raised a large army and marched toward Rome, which was a small city then and did not have many fighting men. Rome hadn't been in great danger before.

The Romans knew that they were not strong enough to meet the Etruscans in open battle. They stayed inside the walls of the city and posted guards on all approaching roads. One morning Porsena's army was seen coming from the hills in the north. Thousands of horsemen and men on foot were marching toward the wooden Sublician Bridge over the Tiber River. The elderly statesmen who governed Rome did not know what to do. They knew if the Etruscan army gained the bridge, it could not be stopped from entering the city.

Among the guards at the bridge was a brave man named Horatius. He was on the other side of the river from the city. When he saw how close the approaching Etruscans were, he called out to the Romans behind him to cut down the bridge. He told them that he and the two men with him would hold back the attacking army. With their shields in front of them and their long spears in their hands, the three men held back the horsemen that Porsena had sent to take the bridge.

The Romans behind them chopped away at the beams and posts supporting the bridge. Their axes rang out, the wood chips flew, and soon the bridge shuddered and was ready to collapse. The men on the bridge called out to Horatius and his two companions to come back across the bridge and save their lives. At that moment, Porsena's horsemen dashed towards them. Horatius told the two guards with him to run for their lives across the bridge while it was still standing. He told them that he would hold the road.

Horatius's companions ran back across the bridge and had barely reached the other side when the sound of crashing beams and timbers could be heard. The bridge toppled over to one side and then fell with a loud splash into the river. When Horatius heard that sound, he knew that the city was safe.

Facing Porsena's men, Horatius moved backward slowly until he was standing on the river bank. A dart thrown by one of the

Etruscan soldiers put out his left eye. Still, he did not falter; he cast his spear at the nearest horseman and then quickly turned around. He could see the white porch of his own home among the trees on the other side of the river.

Horatius leaped into the deep, swift river. Wearing his heavy armor, he sank out of sight. No one expected to see him again. Fortunately, he was a strong man and one of Rome's best swimmers. When he came up, he was halfway across the river and out of range of the spears and darts hurled by Porsena's soldiers.

When Horatius reached the other side, his fellow soldiers stood ready to help him up the river bank. The Romans shouted with pride at brave Horatius's accomplishment as he climbed out of the river. The Etruscans cheered too; they had never seen a man as strong and courageous as Horatius. He had kept them out of Rome, but they did not hesitate to praise him.

The Romans were extremely grateful to Horatius for saving their city. They called him Horatius Cocles, which meant "one-eyed Horatius," because he had lost an eye defending the bridge. The city fathers erected a large brass statue in his honor in the Temple of Vulcan. They awarded him as much land as he could plow around in a single day. For hundreds of years afterward, the people of Rome sang about his bravery in keeping the Etruscans out of their city.

Moral: A determined individual can achieve success in a
       situation that appears hopeless.

Based on: James Baldwin, "Horatius at the Bridge,"
       Favorite Tales of Long Ago

Crossing the Rubicon

In the first century BC, Rome was the most powerful city-state in the world. The Romans had conquered all the countries on the north side of the Mediterranean Sea and most of those on the south side and occupied what is now modern Turkey. Julius Caesar had led a large army into Gaul, the part of Europe that today includes France, Belgium, and Switzerland, and made it a Roman province. He crossed the Rhine River to conquer part of Germany and also established colonies in Britain. He had become the hero of Rome.

For nine years, Caesar had served his republic loyally, but he had enemies at home, those who feared his ambition and envied his achievements. Pompey, the most powerful man in Rome, was one of them. Like Caesar, he commanded a great army, but he had done little to distinguish himself militarily. Pompey made plans to destroy Caesar.

In 49 BC, Caesar's service in Gaul was scheduled to end, and the plan was that he would return to Rome and be elected consul, or ruler, of the Roman Republic. Pompey and his supporters were determined to prevent this, so they convinced the Roman Senate to command Caesar to return to Rome, leaving his army in Gaul. Caesar was told that if he didn't obey this order, he would be considered an enemy of the republic. He knew if he did obey it, false accusations would be made against him. He would be tried for treason, and subsequently not be elected consul.

Caesar called his veteran soldiers together and told them about the plot. They declared their loyalty to him and agreed to go with him to Rome, serving without pay, if necessary. The troops started for Rome with enthusiasm, willing to face any danger. They came to the Rubicon River, a small river in north-central Italy that flowed into the Adriatic Sea and marked the boundary between Cisalpine Gaul and Italy.

By law, Roman magistrates could bring armies into Italy only with the permission of the Senate. Crossing the Rubicon River without that permission was a declaration of war against Pompey and the Senate. Caesar would commit himself to a showdown with Rome itself. This action could involve all of Rome in turmoil.

Caesar hesitated on the banks of the Rubicon. He realized that safety was behind him. Once he crossed the Rubicon into Italy, there was no turning back. When he decided to cross, his decision was irrevocable. News of his crossing was passed along the roads leading to Rome. People turned out to welcome the returning hero. The closer he got to Rome, the more enthusiastic were the celebrations.

Caesar encountered no resistance when he and his army marched through the gates of Rome. Pompey and his supporters had fled. The phrase "crossing the Rubicon" has become known as making a decision from which there is no turning back.

Moral: Occasionally, a decision must be made that is truly irrevocable. Much forethought must be given to such a decision.

Based on: James Baldwin, "Crossing the Rubicon," *Thirty More Famous Stories Retold*

CHAPTER 2

MORAL LEGENDS

"True courage is to do without witnesses everything that one is capable of doing before all the world."

La Rochefoucauld, *Maximes*

The Sacrifice of Aliquipiso

An Oneida Indian village was raided by a band of Mingoes from the north. Mingoes listened to bad spirits and killed everyone and destroyed everything in their path. Oneida women and children abandoned their lodges and fled to the large rocks in the hills, where their braves protected them. The savage marauders searched for days without success for the people of the village.

The Oneidas ran out of food; they feared that if they foraged and hunted, they would be killed. Meeting in council, the warriors and chiefs could think of no solution to their problem. If they remained behind the rocks on the cliff, they would starve; if they ventured out, they would be enslaved or brutally murdered.

A young maiden, Aliquipiso, visited the council of braves and sachems and told them about an idea the Good Spirits had given to her. They told her that if the rocks high on the cliff were rolled into the valley below, everything there would be destroyed. The Good Spirits also told Aliquipiso that if she would lure the plundering Mingoes to the valley below the rocks, they would be killed also. The braves and chiefs were relieved to hear of a solution to their plight. They gave her a necklace of white wampum, made her a princess of the Oneida Nation, and reminded her that she was loved by the Great Spirit.

Aliquipiso left her people in the middle of the night and climbed down from the cliff. The next morning, Mingo scouts found a young maiden wandering lost in the forest. They led Aliquipiso back to the abandoned Oneida village, where they attempted to get her to reveal the hiding place of the Oneidas. They tortured her, but she held out for a long time and won the respect of her captors. Finally, she told the Mingoes that she would lead them to her people. When darkness came, Aliquipiso led her captors to the base of the cliff. Two strong Mingo braves held her in their grasp and were prepared to kill her at the first hint of deception.

The Mingo warriors gathered around Aliquipiso, thinking she was going to show them an opening into a large cave in the cliff. She lifted her head and let out a piercing cry. Above them, the starving Oneida braves pushed the large boulders over the cliff, at her signal. The Mingoes did not have time to get out the way and were crushed under the rocks, along with the Oneida heroine.

Aliquipiso, who was buried near the scene of her courageous sacrifice, was mourned by the Oneidas for many moons. The Great Spirit used her hair to create woodbine, called "running hairs" by the Iroquois, the climbing vine that protects old trees. The Great Spirit changed her body into honeysuckle, which was called "the blood of brave women" by the Oneidas.

Moral: Sacrificing time and effort for others is admirable; sacrificing your life is heroic.

Based on: Arthur C. Parker, *Seneca Myths and Folktales*

The Legend of the Minotaur

This legend begins in Athens, one of the greatest cities in ancient Greece. At the time, however, Athens was a small town perched on top of a cliff. King Aegeus, who ruled Athens in those days, had just welcomed home his son, Theseus, whom he had not seen since birth.

Aegeus was happy to have his son home at last, but Theseus noticed that his father seemed distracted and sad. He also perceived a melancholy among the people of Athens. Mothers were quiet, fathers shook their heads, and children watched the sea all day, as if they expected something fearful to come from it. Many Athenian youths were missing and were said to be visiting relatives in other parts of Greece.

At last Theseus asked his father what troubled the land. Aegeus told his son that he had returned at an unhappy time. A curse so terrible had been placed upon Athens that not even he, Prince Theseus, could deal with it. The trouble dated back to a time when young men came to Athens from all over Greece and other countries to participate in the Panathenaic Festival, which involved contests in distance running, boxing, wrestling, and foot races. Androgeus, the son of King Minos of Crete, was among the victors. He was killed by Athenians, who were jealous of the victories he had won. His comrades left immediately to bear the news to Crete.

The sea was soon black with King Minos's ships seeking vengeance. Minos's army was too powerful for Athens. Athenians went out and begged him for mercy. He said that he would not burn the city or take the people captive. However, he told Athenians that they must pay him a tribute. Every nine years, they must choose by lot seven young men and seven maidens and send them to him. Athens had no choice but to agree. Every nine years a ship with black sails arrived from Crete and took away the captives. This was the ninth year, and the ship was due soon.

Theseus asked what happened to the young people when they reached Crete. Aegeus admitted that they didn't know because none of them had ever returned. However, the sailors of Minos said that the captives were placed in a strange prison, a kind of maze called the Labyrinth. It was full of dark twisting passageways and occupied by a horrible monster called the Minotaur. This creature had the body of a man, the head of a bull, and the teeth of a lion; he devoured everyone that he encountered. Aegeus said he feared that had been the fate of the Athenian youths.

Theseus suggested that they burn the black-sailed ship when it arrived and slay the sailors. Aegeus objected because that would cause Minos to return with his navy and army and destroy Athens. Theseus then asked to be allowed to go as one of the captives, so he could slay the Minotaur. He claimed it as his right as Aegeus's son and heir. Theseus considered it his duty to free Athens from this awful curse.

Aegeus tried to discourage his son from this plan. However, Theseus was determined, and when the ship with the black sails entered the harbor, he joined the doomed group. His father wept when he came to see Theseus off. He asked Theseus that if he did come back alive to lower the black sails as he approached and raise white sails. Aegeus would then know that his son had survived the Labyrinth. Theseus told Aegeus not to worry but to look for white sails, since he would return in triumph.

The ship put to sea and reached Crete after sailing for many days. The Athenian prisoners were marched into the palace, where King Minos sat on his throne, surrounded by courtiers clothed in silken robes and ornaments of gold. Minos fixed his eyes on Theseus. Theseus bowed and met the king's gaze. Minos observed that the captives were fifteen in number, but that his tribute claimed only fourteen.

Theseus told him that he had come of his own will. Minos asked him why, and he said that the people of Athens wanted to be free. Minos agreed that if Theseus slew the Minotaur, Athens would be absolved of the tribute. Theseus said that he planned to slay the Minotaur, causing a stir in the court. A beautiful young woman glided among them and stood just behind the throne. This was Ariadne, Minos's daughter, a wise and tender-hearted maiden. Theseus bowed low and then stood erect with his eyes on the face of Ariadne.

Minos told Theseus that he spoke like a king's son, perhaps someone who had never known hardship. Theseus replied that he had known hardship and that his name was Theseus, Aegeus's son. He asked the king to let him face the Minotaur alone. If he could not slay it, his companions would follow him into the Labyrinth.

Minos responded that if Aegeus's son wanted to die alone, he could do so.

The Athenian youths were led upstairs and along galleries, each to a chamber more rich and beautiful than they had seen before, even in their dreams. Each was taken to a bath, washed and clothed in new garments, and then treated to a lavish feast. None of them had sufficient appetite to eat, except Theseus, who knew he would need his strength.

That evening, as Theseus was preparing for bed, he heard a soft knock on his door. Suddenly, Ariadne, the king's daughter, was standing in his room. Once again Theseus gazed into her eyes and saw there a kind of strength and compassion that he had never encountered before. She told Theseus that too many of his countrymen had disappeared in the Labyrinth, and that she had brought him a dagger and could show him and his friends the way to escape. He thanked her for the dagger but said that he couldn't flee. He was going to take on the Minotaur.

Ariadne warned Theseus that even if he could slay the Minotaur, he would have to find his way out of the Labyrinth. She told him that it had many dark twists and turns and so many dead ends and false passages that not even her father knew its secrets. She took from her gown a spool of thread and pressed it into his hand. She said that if he were determined to go forward with his plan he should tie the end to a stone as soon as he entered the Labyrinth and unwind the thread as he wandered through the maze. The thread would guide him out.

Theseus looked at her, not knowing what to say. He asked why she was doing this, knowing that she would be in trouble if her father found out. She told him that if she didn't, he and his friends would be in greater danger. Theseus knew then that he loved her.

The next morning Theseus was led to the Labyrinth. As soon as the guards had shut him inside, he tied one end of the thread to a rock. He began to walk slowly, keeping a firm grip on the precious string. He went down the widest corridor, from which others turned off to the left and to the right, until he came to a wall. He retraced his steps, tried another hallway, and then another, always listening for the monster.

Theseus passed through many dark winding passageways, gradually descending further and further into the Labyrinth. Finally he reached a room that was piled high with bones, and he knew he was near the beast. Theseus sat still and from far away heard a sound, like the echo of a roar. He stood up and listened intently. The sound, like that of a bull but thinner, came nearer and nearer. Theseus scooped up a handful of dirt from the floor and drew his dagger with the other hand.

The roars of the Minotaur came nearer and nearer. Theseus could hear the thudding of feet along the floor. He squeezed into a corner of the passageway and crouched there. His heart was pounding. Catching sight of him, the Minotaur roared and rushed straight at him. Theseus leaped up and, dodging aside, threw the handful of dirt into the monster's eyes. The Minotaur, shrieking and confused, rubbed his eyes. Theseus crept up behind the beast and slashed at his legs. The Minotaur fell with a crash, biting at the floor with his lion's teeth.

Theseus waited for his chance and then plunged the dagger into the Minotaur's heart three times. He kneeled and thanked all the gods. When he finished his prayer, he hacked off the head of the Minotaur. Clutching the monster's head, he followed the thread out of the Labyrinth. It seemed that he would never find his way out of those dark, gloomy passageways. It took so long he wondered if the string had snapped somewhere, and he had lost his way. Finally he came to the entrance and fell to the ground, worn out from his struggle.

Minos was surprised when he saw the Minotaur's head in the grip of Theseus. The king kept his word, however, and gave Theseus and his friends the freedom he had promised. Minos wished for peace between Crete and Athens and bade Theseus and his friends farewell.

Theseus knew that he owed his life and his country's freedom to Ariadne's courage. He felt that he could not leave Crete without her. One version of the legend is that Theseus asked Minos for his daughter's hand in marriage, and that the king consented. Another version has Ariadne stealing aboard the departing ship at the last moment without her father's knowledge. Either way, the two lovers were together when the anchor lifted and the dark ship sailed from Crete.

Unfortunately, this happy ending is mixed with tragedy, as legends sometimes are. The Cretan captain of the vessel did not know that he was supposed to hoist white sails if Theseus came home in triumph. King Aegeus, as he anxiously watched from a high cliff, saw the black sails coming over the horizon. The thought of losing his son broke his heart. He fell from the towering cliff into the sea, which is now called the Aegean Sea.

Moral: Courage is required to right a wrong. Compassion can guide courage.

Based on: Andrew Lang, "The Minotaur"

Citizen William Tell

Centuries ago, men came out of the valleys around Lake Lucerne in the heart of the Swiss Alps to forge an alliance and to swear loyalty to it. The Switzerland of today grew out of that alliance. The inhabitants of those valleys fought many fierce battles against the powerful foreign lords of their land, the ruling nobles and princes, before freedom was won. One of the bravest fighters for the freedom of Switzerland was William Tell.

William Tell was a chamois hunter, a quiet man who usually shunned the society of his fellows. He lived near Altdorf in the canton of Uri. When hunting chamois, Tell carried his bow on his back. He seldom missed a shot; he was the best bowman in the valley. He sold his chamois skins to the market in Lucerne and with his earnings lived a humble, contented, and secluded life with his family.

Gessler, the tyrannical Austrian bailiff of Uri, ruled with an iron hand. Tension had existed between the Swiss and the Austrians since long before 1315, when a Swiss force defeated the large Austrian army advancing from Zug to Schwyz at Morgarten, laying the foundations of Swiss liberty.

One day Gessler thought of a new way to antagonize the free peasants who resisted his rule. He directed his men to place a hat on top of a pole in the marketplace of Altdorf. He ordered that every grown man that walked by it must kneel down and pay homage to the hat, as if it were the bailiff or the Emperor himself. Two armed soldiers were assigned to guard the pole and the hat and to enforce the bailiff's order. Villagers went out of their way to avoid walking by the hat.

This order of the bailiff, to kneel down before an empty hat, filled the people with indignation. On November 8, 1307, the leaders of the three cantons, or forest districts, around Lake Lucerne met one night on the Rutli, a lonely pasture in the forest above the lake, to make a plan to rid themselves of their foreign oppressors and set their country free. Werner von Stauffacher of Schwyz, Walter Furst of Uri, and Arnold von Melchthal of Unterwalden, each with ten companions, including William Tell, met to form the plan. They agreed to storm the fortresses after dark on the coming New Year's Eve to drive out the bailiffs.

One day soon after these meetings, William Tell came into the marketplace of Altdorf, holding his bow in his right hand and his young son with his left hand. The men of Uri admired him as a fellow citizen and a champion archer. Tell walked by the hat on the pole without kneeling. The two guards seized him and told him he would go to prison for disobeying the bailiff's order. He thrust the guards aside and told them that he was a free man. He knelt before God, he bowed his head before the Emperor and his representatives, but he would not pay homage to an empty hat.

At that moment Gessler entered the square with a retinue of several dozen heavily armed soldiers. The citizens of Altdorf came into the marketplace to support Tell. Tell told them to stay calm and not to get into trouble over him. Many of those who had sworn the oath at Rutli were there. Tell and Gessler faced each other in silence. Gessler hated Tell, one of the leaders of the free men opposing his plans.

Gessler ordered Tell to be thrown in prison for disobeying his orders. Tell responded that the citizens were free men, and that they didn't have to pay reverence to an empty hat. Gessler saw that Tell carried his bow with him, which was against the law. Gessler told Tell that he would be punished for being armed.

Gessler commanded his guards, "Seize Tell's son and stand him under the linden tree. Place this apple on the boy's head and measure eighty paces away from him. You, Tell, draw your bow. You are to shoot the apple off the boy's head. If you hit your mark, I will let you go free. If you miss the mark, then you shall die, both you and your son."

Tell looked at Gessler with horror in his eyes. Rage seized him; he wanted to rush at the bailiff and drag him off his horse. Then he thought of his son. The threat of death was hanging over his head too. He forced himself to kneel down and to ask the bailiff's pardon. He said, "I am a simple man. It was not out of ill will that I disobeyed your order. Forgive me, and let me go." The boy's grandfather also stepped forward, kneeled before the hated tyrant, and pleaded on behalf of his son. The bailiff was not moved.

Gessler's men positioned Tell's son under the linden tree and began to blindfold him. The boy refused the blindfold, telling them that he was not afraid of his father's arrow. Tell took aim. A deadly silence fell over the entire square. Tell dropped his arm holding the bow and said that he could not do it.

The bailiff looked at him mockingly. He told Tell that if he could carry arms illegally and disobey his order to kneel before the hat, then he could so this, too. The bailiff reminded him that if he didn't shoot, both he and his son would die.

An uncanny calm took possession of Tell. He measured the distance between himself and the boy and then between himself and Gessler. He placed one arrow into position in his bow and took a second arrow out of his quiver and stuck it in his belt. He took aim and shot the arrow. It split the apple in half. A thousand townspeople shouted with delight. The valley folk embraced one another with joy. They began to carry Tell away.

Gessler ordered his men to drive the people back. He congratulated Tell that it had been a master shot and asked what the purpose of the second arrow was. Tell hesitated until the bailiff assured him that whatever he had to say, his life was not at stake. Tell then answered that the second arrow was for Gessler; if he had missed the apple and killed this own child, the bailiff would have been the next target. Tell said that he wouldn't have missed.

Gessler turned pale. He directed his men to put Tell in chains and said, "Take him to my fortress at Kussnacht. The walls there are more than three feet thick. He shall lie in the deepest dungeon and never see the sun or moonlight again. He shall live on but in such a life that he would rather be dead. I will see to it that I am safe from his arrows." The boy clung to his father's arm and begged him not to go. The grandfather had to drag the boy away from his father. The old man's heart was broken. Tell showed no fear.

Gessler's boat was waiting in the harbor. It was the bailiff's official boat with eight pairs of oars. Tell was flung down in the middle of the boat; he was chained and well guarded. Gessler thought that Tell would never be able to harm him again. Gessler and his soldiers rowed out into the lake, which was surrounded by mountains and ravines.

Tell looked up at the sky. A bank of clouds was moving in from the south. He knew what that meant: a foehn, a warm, unhealthy wind that brought sudden storms. The air was heavy, and gradually the sky grew dark. Suddenly violent gusts of wind blew out onto the lake from the valleys. The gusts whipped up the waves, which struck the boat with increasing force. Two oars splintered like matchsticks. The tremendous waves jerked the helm out of the steersman's hands, and the boat rocked back and forth at the mercy of the storm.

Gessler and his men were pale with fear. They were afraid that the boat might be shattered into fragments on the rocks. The helmsman turned to the bailiff and said, "We are in great danger. We have lost control of the boat. There is only one hope for us and that lies with Tell. With his great strength and experience, he might be able to hold the helm. Let him be unchained so that he can help us."

Tell was unfettered and took the helm. He told the oarsmen to row with their utmost strength. He promised that the lake would be calmer on the other side of the large rock ledge extending out into the lake toward which he was steering. The oarsmen took heart again and rowed with all their might. Finally the boat reached the small peninsula of rock.

Tell knew it well. A flat rock ten feet wide ran out from it just above the level of the water. In later years, this rock became known as Tell's Platte. Great waves were breaking over the rock. Tell's face was rigid. He grasped the helm firmly and jammed it back, causing the boat to jerk around violently and face the open lake. He grabbed his bow and arrows and leaped out of the boat onto the flat rock.

Gessler sprang from his seat but was thrown down again by a large wave. Tell plunged into the thick undergrowth and was quickly out of sight. Without a helmsman, the boat tossed helplessly on the waters.

Tell knew that Gessler would try to land at Brunnen, a nearby village on the lake, and that he would ride from there to his fortress at Kussnacht. Tell knew all the trails and footpaths and wound his way through the forest until he was within sight of Brunnen and the canton of Schwyz. He stopped to eat at the Sust Tavern in Brunnen and heard that the bailiff's boat had survived the storm and landed at the village dock. It was time to act.

Tell chose a footpath that led through the thick forest. He walked all night and by morning was near the only approach to the bailiff's fortress, a deep, narrow gorge with thick shrubs on both sides of the trail. There he hid and waited for the bailiff. Eventually he saw Gessler. Tell drew his bow and shot an arrow that pierced the bailiff's heart. Gessler's last sight was Tell standing tall above him. Tell evaded Gessler's men and headed for home.

The news traveled fast to the canton of Uri that the bailiff was dead and could no longer ravage the country or torment the peasants. The men of Uri crowded into the streets of the small towns and discussed the events with unsuppressed excitement. When Tell entered Altdorf, his friends flocked around him and greeted him with shouts of joy as their rescuer and deliverer. He left the crowds, with his wife at his side, to return home.

On the morning of New Year's Day, 1308, Tell got up at dawn and climbed the hills to hunt chamois. From the heights, he looked down on Altdorf. Where the fortress had stood the day before, smoke was now rising from a heap of ruins.

The people of Altdorf had left few stones of the fortress standing. William Tell's deed had been a signal to the men from the other cantons to begin their fight for freedom. They stormed the other fortresses and drove the Emperor's representatives out of the country.

The three cantons set up a common system of law and administration. They vowed never to submit to a foreign judge or overlord and to support each other with life-and-death loyalty. The Switzerland of today grew out of the old Deeds of Confederation, drawn up by the three valley cantons and the cantons that joined them.

After William Tell died, the men of Uri came to Tell's house and asked for his bow. They said, "This shall be kept forever and handed down to our children and grandchildren. It shall remind us that courage, daring, and selfless devotion laid the foundation of our Confederation, and that these things have made it strong." Over time citizen William Tell became a national hero of the Swiss people.

Moral: The collective good cannot be obtained without courage and determination among those allied to the cause.

Based on: Fritz Muller-Guggenbuhl, "William Tell and the Swiss Confederation," *Swiss-Alpine Folk-Tales*

The Bravery of Arnold von Winkelried

The union of the cantons and cities of the republic of Switzerland has been a remarkable facet of history. Of different ethnicities, languages, and religions—unalike in habits, tastes, opinions, and costumes—they have, nevertheless, held together by pressure from without, and a spirit of patriotism has kept the mountainous republic whole for centuries.

Originally the lands had been fiefs of the Holy Roman Empire. The Emperor was the lord of the cities. The great family of Hapsburg, who became hereditary rulers of the Empire, were in reality Swiss; the county that gave them their title was in the canton of Aargau. Rodolf of Hapsburg was elected leader of the burghers of Zurich long before he was chosen to lead the Empire. He remained Swiss at heart, retaining his mountaineer's open simplicity and honesty to the end of his life. The country was loyal and prosperous during his reign.

Unfortunately, his son Albert permitted those tyrannies of his bailiffs that goaded the Swiss to their celebrated revolt and began the long series of wars with the House of Hapsburg—or, as it was called later, Austria—that finally established Switzerland's independence.

On one side the Dukes of Austria, with their ponderous German chivalry, wanted to reduce the cantons and cities of the Swiss to vassalage, not to the Imperial Crown, a distant and scarcely felt obligation, but to the Duchy of Austria. On the other side, the hardy Swiss peasants and sturdy burghers understood their true position: Austrian control would expose their young men to fighting in the Dukes' wars, cause demands to be made on their property, and fill their hills with castles for ducal bailiffs who would be no more than licensed robbers. It was not surprising that the generations of William Tell and Arnold von Winkelried bequeathed a resolute purpose of resistance to their descendants.

In 1386, many years after the first assertion of Swiss independence, Leopold the Handsome, Duke of Austria, a bold but overly proud and violent prince, involved himself in a quarrel with the Swiss concerning insulting tolls and tributes imposed upon the cities near the Austrian border. A bitter war broke out, and men of the Swiss city of Lucerne attacked the customhouse at Rothenburg, where the tolls had been particularly heavy. Lucerne admitted the cities of Sempach and Richensee to their league.

Leopold and all the neighboring nobles joined forces. They were spurred on by their hatred and contempt for the Swiss, whom they considered low-born and presumptuous. In one day the Duke received twenty pledges of support in his march against Sempach and Lucerne. He sent Johann Bonstetten with a large force in the direction of Zurich and led his own men, mounted and on foot, to advance on Sempach. Zurich undertook its own defense, and the forest cantons sent their brave peasants to support Lucerne and Sempach.

Leopold's troops rode around the walls of Sempach, hurling insults at the inhabitants. Leopold taunted Sempach with the reckless destruction his men caused by destroying the surrounding fields. He shouted, "Send a breakfast to the reapers." From the city walls, the burgomaster pointed to the woods in the distance where his allies were hiding and answered, "My masters of Lucerne and their friends will bring it."

The Duke's wiser friends, including the Baron von Hasenberg, suggested waiting until they were joined by the troops of Bonstetten, who had gone towards Zurich. This prudent counsel was ignored by the younger knights, who boasted that they would deliver up this handful of villains by noon.

The story of that July 9, 1386, battle was told by one of the burghers named Tchudi, who fought in the ranks of Lucerne. He was a brave warrior and a storyteller. His ballad was translated by another storyteller, Sir Walter Scott:

> And thus to each other said,
> Yon handful down to hew
> Will be no boastful tale to tell,
> The peasants are so few.

The Duke's men were drawn up in a solid, compact body, presenting an unbroken line of spears that projected beyond their wall of shields and polished armor. The Swiss were not only few in number, but armor was scarce among them. Some had boards fastened on their arms as shields, and some had halberds that had been used by their forefathers at the battle of Morgarten in 1315, which had laid the foundations of Swiss liberty. Still others had two-handed swords and battle-axes. The Swiss drew themselves up in the shape of a wedge.

> The gallant Swiss confederates then
> They prayed to God aloud,
> And He displayed His rainbow fair,
> Against a swarthy cloud.

The villagers rushed against the tightly packed spears of the Austrians, but in vain. The banner of Lucerne was in the most danger. Their leader was killed along with sixty of his men, and no Austrians had been wounded. The flanks of the Austrians began to advance to enclose the small peasant force and destroy it. In a moment of danger and stillness, a voice was heard. Arnold von Winkelried of Unterwalden, with the determination of a man who dares all things, saw the only way to save his country and shouted, "I will open a passage."

> I have a virtuous wife at home,
> A wife and infant son.
> I leave them to my country's care
> The field shall yet be won!
> He rushed against the Austrian band
> In desperate career,
> And with his body, breast, and hand,
> Bore down each hostile spear
> Four lances splintered on his crest,
> Six shivered in his side,
> Still the serried files he pressed,
> He broke their ranks and died!

The very weight of the desperate charge of this courageous man opened a breach in the line of spears. In rushed the Swiss wedge, and the weight of the Austrian nobles' armor and the length of their spears were only an encumbrance. They began to fall before the Swiss blows, and Duke Leopold was urged to flee. He said, "I would rather die honorably than live with dishonor."

Leopold saw his standard-bearer struck to the ground and

seized the banner and waved it over his head. He threw himself into
the thickest throng of his enemy. His body was found among a heap
of dead soldiers. No less than 2,000 of his force died with him, of
whom a third were counts, barons, and knights.

> Then lost was banner, spear, and shield
>   At Sempach in the flight;
> The cloister vaults at Konigsfeld
>   Hold many an Austrian knight.

The Swiss lost only 200, but, since they were tired from the
heat of the July sun, they did not pursue their enemy. They gave
thanks to the God of victories, and the next day they buried the
dead. They carried Duke Leopold and twenty-seven of his most
illustrious companions to the Abbey of Konigsfeld. They buried
him in the old tomb of his forefathers, the lords of Aargau, who had
been interred there in the days before the House of Hapsburg had
grown arrogant with success.

Every July 9, Swiss people assemble on the battlefield around
four stone crosses that mark the site. A priest gives a thanksgiving
sermon on the victory that ensured the freedom of Switzerland, and
another reads the roll of the brave 200, who, after Winkelried's
example, gave their lives for the cause. The congregation then proceeds to a small battle-chapel, the walls of which are painted with
the deed of Arnold von Winkelried and the distinguished achievements of other confederates. Masses are said for the slain. It is not
surprising that men nurtured in the memory of such actions were
among the most trusted soldiery in Europe, for example, the Swiss
guards at the Vatican.

Moral: One man or woman can make a difference, especially when
        that person is completely unselfish.

Based on: Charlotte Mary Yonge, "The Battle of Sempach,"
        A Book of Golden Deeds of All Times and All Lands

The Little Hero of Holland

Much of the land in Holland lies below sea level. Since the level of the land is lower than that of the sea, the water is held back by great walls, called dikes, to keep the North Sea from rushing in and flooding farms and villages. For centuries the Dutch people have worked hard to keep the dikes strong and their land safe. Everyone, including children, watches the walls regularly because a small leak can rapidly grow into a large leak that might cause a disastrous flood.

Years ago a young boy named Peter lived in the city of Haarlem in Holland. Peter's father tended the gates in the dikes, called sluices, which allowed ships to pass between Holland's canals and the North Sea. One autumn day when Peter was eight years old, he walked across the top of the dike near his home to visit his grand-mother.

Peter's mother had told him to be home before dark, so he start-ed for home just before sunset. He ran along the top of the dike because he had stayed at his grandmother's cottage longer than he had intended. He realized that he was going to be late for supper. Farmers working in nearby fields had all finished their work and left for home. Peter could hear the waves beating against the great wall. Recent rains had caused the water level to rise.

Suddenly Peter heard a noise—the sound of trickling water. He stopped and looked down the side of the dike to find the source of the noise. He saw a small hole in the dike, through which a thin but steady stream of water was flowing. He realized that it would not take long for the small hole to become a large one. He looked around for something with which to plug the hole, but he could find nothing.

Peter reached down and stuck his forefinger into the tiny hole in the dike, and the flow of water stopped. He called for help as loudly as he could. No one was around to hear, however; everyone was home at supper. Soon night fell, and it became much colder. Peter continued to call out for help. He hoped that someone would walk across the dike that evening to visit a friend. No one came.

Peter's mother looked for him along the dike many times and finally closed and locked the cottage door. She assumed that Peter had decided to stay overnight with his grandmother, as he had done many times. Peter thought of his brother and sister in their warm beds, but he was not going to abandon his responsibility. He did not sleep that night. He was grateful that the moon and stars provided light.

Early the next morning a man walking along the top of the dike on his way to work heard a groan. He looked over the edge of the wall and saw Peter, who was weary and aching from his vigil. He asked Peter if he was hurt. Peter told him that he was holding the water back and asked him to go for help. The alarm was spread, and men came running to repair the hole. Peter was carried home, and the word spread in Haarlem and beyond of the brave little hero of Holland.

Moral: By being responsible and unselfish, an individual can
        protect the many.

Based on: J. Berg Esenwein and Marietta Stockard,
        "The Little Hero of Haarlem,"
        Children's Stories and How to Tell Them

CHAPTER 3

LUMINARIES / NOTABLES

"Courage is the best gift of all; courage stands before everything. It is what preserves our liberty, safety, life, and our homes and parents, our country and children. courage comprises all things: a man with courage has every blessing."

Plautus, *Amphitruo*

ST. PAUL THE APOSTLE (AD 5-57) Apostle of the Gentiles

"And immediately, he proclaimed Jesus in the synagogues, saying, 'He is the Son of God.' And all who heard him were amazed and said 'Is this not the man who made havoc in Jerusalem of those who called upon this name?' . . . but Saul [Paul] increased all the more in strength, and confounded the Jews who lived in Damascus by proving that Jesus was the Christ."

Acts 9:20-22

Paul's Jewish name was Saul. As a Roman citizen, his Latin name was Paul. Jews, in Paul's early years, had two names, one in Hebrew and one in Latin or Greek. Paul was born in 5 AD to a devout Jewish family in the city of Tarsus, which was a center for trade on the coast of the Mediterranean Sea. At the time, Tarsus was considered the most influential city in Asia Minor.

Paul was educated in the Hillel school in Jerusalem. He received a broad education in classical literature, ethics, and philosophy. As noted in the New Testament, Paul actively persecuted the early Christians in Jerusalem.

Paul's conversion to Christianity occurred on the road to Damascus when, between the years 31 and 36, he had a vision of the resurrected Jesus. According to the Acts of the Apostles: "Paul heard a voice saying to him, Saul, Saul, why persecutest thou me? Saul replied, Who art thou, Lord? And the Lord said, I am Jesus whom thou persecutest. The resurrected Jesus appeared to him in a great light. He was struck blind but, after three days, his sight was restored by Ananias of Damascus, and Paul was baptized and began to preach that Jesus of Nazareth is the Jewish Messiah and the Son of God." Paul had the courage of his convictions.

Paul went on three missionary journeys. On his first trip, he went from Antioch to Cyprus and to southern Asia Minor. He then returned to Antioch, which was a principal hub for his evangelism. Paul remained in Antioch for a long time with his disciples. He traveled with one or more disciples, initially with Barnabas, then John Mark, Silas, and others.

In autumn 49, on his second missionary journey, Paul and his traveling companion, Barnabas, traveled from Jerusalem around the Mediterranean Sea to Antioch. He visited Tarsus, his birthplace, and then Lystra and Philippi, where he was jailed. An earthquake caused the gates of the prison to collapse. Paul did not escape but remained in the jail. This motivated his jailer to convert to Christianity. Next, he traveled to Berea and on to Athens. He continued on to Corinth, where he stayed eighteen months between 50 and 52. In 52, he stopped at Cenchreae before sailing to Ephesus and on to Caesarea and north to Antioch, where he stayed for a year.

On his third missionary journey, Paul traveled around the region of Galatia to teach and strengthen the believers. He moved on to Phrygia, an early hub of Christianity, where he stayed for three years, working as a tentmaker as he had done earlier in Corinth.

Paul traveled through Macedonia to Archea. He stayed in Greece for three months. He wrote his Epistle to the Romans during this time. He moved on to Illyricum in the Roman Province of Macedonia. On their way to Jerusalem, Paul and his companions went to Phillipi, Troas, Militus, Rhodes, and Tyre. His last stop before Jerusalem was Caesarea, where he and his companions stayed with Philip the Evangelist.

After Paul completed his third missionary journey in 57, he made his last visit to Jerusalem. Initially, he was warmly received. After a week in Jerusalem, however, he was accused of being "against the Law." Some Jews from Roman Asia accused him of defiling the temple by bringing gentiles into it. He was dragged out of the temple by an incensed mob. He narrowly escaped being killed before he was arrested by Roman centurions.

Paul was taken to Caesarea Maritima and imprisoned for two years. In 59, a new governor reopened his case. Paul used his right as a Roman citizen to appeal to Caesar. He and his companions sailed for Rome where Paul would stand trial for his supposed crimes.

Paul was shipwrecked off Malta, where the citizens treated him kindly. From Malta, he traveled to Rome by way of Syracuse, Rhegium, and Puteoli, arriving in Rome in 60. He spent two years under house arrest, preaching from his home. It is thought that from his time in Rome, Paul traveled to Spain to preach the Gospel.

The date of Paul's death is not certain but is thought to be prior to the death of Nero in in 68. Paul died by being beheaded. It was thought that he was buried outside the wall of Rome on the Via Laurentina.

In 2002, a marble sarcophagus, inscribed with the words "PAULO APOSTOLO MART" (Paul apostle martyr) was found during excavations outside the walls of the Basilica of Saint Paul on the Via Ostiensis. In 2005, the Vatican declared this to be the tomb of St. Paul.

In 2009, Pope Benedict XVI revealed the excavation findings. The sarcophagus was not opened but was examined with a probe, revealing incense, blue and purple linen, and bone fragments. The bone was carbon-dated to the first or second century. The Vatican announced that the findings support the conclusion that the tomb is St. Paul's.

E. P. Sanders, in *St. Paul, the Apostle,* observed: " Paul's influence on Christian thinking arguably has been more significant than any other New Testament author." In *Reinventing Paul*, John G. Gager stated that "Paul was installed as the center of the New Testament precisely because he, like the later Christian communities that shaped these Christian scriptures and produced the New Testament, shared their rejection-replacement view of Judaism."

According to John Pollock in *The Apostle,* at the time of his death, Paul said: "Who shall separate us from the love of Christ? Shall tribulation . . . or sword? I reckon that the sufferings of the present time are not worthy to be compared with the glory."

SIR CHRISTOPHER WREN (1632-1723) Architect of St. Paul's Cathedral

"Courage is generosity of the highest order, for the brave are prodigal of the most precious things."

C. C. Colton, *Lacon,Vol. 1*

Christopher Wren was born on October 20, 1632, during the reign of Charles I. His father, Christopher Wren, Sr., was Rector of East Knoyle, Wiltshire. Soon after his son's birth, Christopher, Sr., succeeded his brother Matthew as Dean of Windsor and Registrar of the Order of the Garter. The brothers had ties to the court, and both suffered for being High Church and Royalists during the Civil War. Dean Christopher's house was sacked twice, causing him to move to West Country and then to seek refuge with his son-in-law, William Holder. Matthew was imprisoned for eighteen years in the Tower of London.

The Civil War broke out when young Christopher was ten years old. He studied at Westminster School with the highly regarded headmaster, Dr. Busby. Christopher, a serious student, wrote a letter to his father from Westminster School containing the message, "What in me lies I will perform, as much as I am able lest these gifts should have been bestowed on an ungrateful soul. May the good God Almighty be with me in my undertakings.... "

Wren attended Wadham College, Oxford, in the late 1640s and was awarded a B.A. degree in 1651. In 1654, he was a fellow at All Souls College when diarist John Evelyn referred to him as "that miracle of a youth, Mr. Christopher Wren." At that time, considerable overlap existed between the arts and sciences. Wren had a good classical education and was well versed in Latin; astronomy was his principal academic interest. In 1657, he was appointed Professor of Astronomy at Gresham College, London. His other interests included the study of the laws of motion, meteorology, optics, and physiology.

In 1657, Wren attended a series of scientific meetings at Gresham College. The attendees formed a society in 1660 that was granted a King's Charter as the Royal Society the following year and evolved into the most distinguished international scientific society of its time. In 1661, Wren succeeded Dr. Seth Ward, his teacher at Oxford, as the Savilian Professor of Astronomy. Later that year, Wren was honored with a Doctor of Laws degree by Oxford University.

King Charles II visited Oxford, and Wren organized a Philosophical Society program for him in which Wren made his first direct reference to the field of architecture. In 1663, the King appointed Wren assistant to Sir John Denham, the Surveyor-General of Works. Denham was a failure as an architect. John Evelyn observed of Denham, "I knew him to be a better poet than architect, although he had Mr. Webb to assist him." John Webb was noted architect Inigo Jones's assistant and married his daughter. Jones was the dominant English architect prior to Wren. Working under Denham, Wren became the Surveyor-General of Works in fact if not in name.

Wren's efforts shifted from other scientific pursuits to architecture. His first architectural endeavor was the chapel at Pembroke College, Cambridge, followed by his design for the Sheldonian Theatre at Oxford.

During the summer of 1665, Wren received an invitation to visit the Earl of St. Alban's, the English Ambassador to France, in Paris. Wren's first trip to the Continent gave him the opportunity to view its architecture. He made daily visits to the Louvre, which was under construction at the time, and was impressed by the College of the Four Nations (University of Paris and its four colleges: Arts, Law, Medicine, and Theology.)

Wren was introduced to François Mansart, who did the initial designs for the Sorbonne and the Church of Val-de-Grâce, and to Giovanni Bernini, who showed him his architectural design for the Louvre. Bernini, an extremely successful sculptor and architect, believed that "in order to excel in the arts, one must rise above all the rules and create a manner peculiar to oneself." Wren visited Fontainebleau and the Palace at Versailles as well as many villas, including Chantilly, Constances, Le Raincy, Liancour, Maisons, Ruel, Vaux, and Verneuil.

When he returned from the continent, Wren, as Deputy Surveyor-General, was appointed to a commission overseeing the repair of St. Paul's Cathedral, which was the second church on that site. The first St. Paul's, which had been built in the mid-seventh century, burned down in 1087. Late in the thirteenth century, construction of its replacement still hadn't been completed. During the reign of King Stephen, the cathedral was again destroyed by fire. Reconstruction began immediately. The medieval Cathedral was rebuilt with a Gothic choir and a Romanesque nave. In the 1630s, Inigo Jones had recased the nave using pilasters instead of buttresses and had constructed a Corinthian portico at the west end of the Cathedral.

The older members of the Commission, Sir John Denham, Sir Roger Pratt, and John Webb, recommended repairing the existing Cathedral, but Wren suggested sweeping changes. He suggested refacing the inside of the nave as well as the outside and replacing the nave vault with saucer domes. Wren's proposals for St. Paul's all contained two principal components—a great central area and a high dome. His proposals encountered considerable opposition but were finally agreed upon.

However, an even more drastic change faced St. Paul's. Beginning on September 2, 1667, the Great Fire raged for three days, leveling most of the Cathedral as well as destroying or virtually destroying eighty-seven other churches. John Evelyn noted that "the stones of St. Paul's flew like grenades, the melting lead running down the streets in a stream, the very pavements of them glowing with fiery redness."

Wren was one of three members of a Commission appointed by the King to make recommendations on rebuilding London; the City also appointed three members. By September 11, Wren had completed plans for London that would have replaced the old narrow, winding streets with an orderly layout of streets radiating from a civic center where the Royal Exchange is located today. The plan included a civic center surrounded by buildings for "Ensurances," the Excise Office, the Mint, and the Post Office.

Before the plan could be executed, however, citizens who had lost their homes and had no place to live began to rebuild on the old foundations. All that the Commission accomplished was to institute the Rebuilding Act of 1667, which prohibited building timber houses and houses with upper stories overhanging the street. This Act reduced the hazard of fire in the future, but did nothing to make London a well-laid-out city.

Wren's next designs were for the Chapel of Emmanuel College, Cambridge, in 1668 and, a year later, the Customs House, which was destroyed by fire in the early 1700s. Sir John Denham died in 1669, and Wren was appointed Surveyor-General to succeed him. Also that year, Wren married Faith Coghill, the daughter of Sir Thomas Coghill of Bletchingdon, whom he had known as a youth. They had a son, Christopher, who was only seven months old when Faith died in 1675 of smallpox. In 1677, Wren married Jane Fitzwilliam, the sister of Lord Fitzwilliam of Lifford. They had two children, Jane and William.

Paying for the rebuilding of London and St. Paul's was a challenge. The country was bankrupt; nevertheless, it had to find a way to rebuild the city for the hundred thousand homeless. Money also had to be made available to support the Royal Navy, whose ships anchored in the Medway were being attacked by the Dutch. Economy was foremost, and Wren would have to find a way to finance the rebuilding of St. Paul's.

Most of the other members of the Commission wanted to patch and repair the Cathedral. Wren knew that structural problems in the Cathedral existed even before the Great Fire; he knew that rebuilding was the only way to proceed. He observed, "Since we cannot mend this great Ruine we will not disfigure it." From this point onward, he would struggle with his strong feelings for his art and doing what he knew was right despite the ongoing resistance of those who wanted to economize.

Wren oversaw the demolition of the remnants of the old St. Paul's, which began in 1667 and continued for two years. He supervised the first use of gunpowder in demolition. Unfortunately, in Wren's absence, his crew used twice the amount of gunpowder in the second demolition effort. No one was killed, but the residents of the area were terrified by the flying debris. Wren wasn't permitted to use gunpowder again. The last columns had to be knocked down with a battering ram.

In 1669, Wren was commissioned to rebuild the Temple Bar, the gateway from Westminster to the City of London. This right of way had been maintained by the Mayor of London and the Corporation for almost 400 years. Wren's design of the Temple Bar was constructed of stone with a large central arch and a guard room containing recesses with statues of Charles I and Charles II on one side and of James I and Queen Elizabeth on the other. In 1872, the Temple Bar was moved to Theobald's Park to alleviate traffic congestion.

The first two churches that Wren rebuilt after the Great Fire were St. Christopher-le-Stocks, which was later torn down when the Bank of England was built, and St. Mary-le-Bow, which was destroyed in the air raids of World War II. Then he returned his attention to St. Paul's. In addition to the design approved before the Great Fire, Wren had prepared several designs with a classic dome in the center of the old Gothic Cathedral. In *Wren: His Work and Times*, John Lindsey commented on the next design:

> Then followed Wren's own favorite design, one of incomparable beauty, in the form of a Greek Cross, with a vestibule and portico, surmounted by a lesser dome, the points of the Greek Cross being connected by concave facades. The King was so taken by this design that he ordered a huge model to be made of it (which still exists). But the Chapter and other Clergy thought the model not enough of a cathedral fashion, in that the choir was designed circular, and there were no regular aisles or nave.
>
> Over these points the architect and the Chapter fought bitterly, Wren being reminded that "his" cathedral must conform as nearly as possible to the designs of other cathedrals and that side aisles

51

were an absolute necessity if the processions in the cathedral were to have that dignity to which they had been used. Wren, grumbling that "they are impertinent, our Religion not using Processions" reluctantly abandoned the design and produced another, irreverently known as the "Nightmare" design.

The King approved this plan, but fortunately he allowed Wren "liberty in the prosecution of his work, to make some variations, rather ornamental than essential, as from time to time he should see proper, and to leave the whole to his management."

Wren availed himself of this permission to an incredible extent, and constructed a building almost as different from the approved plan as St. Paul's Cathedral is from that of Salisbury.

Financing the construction was an ongoing problem. Clearly, rebuilding St. Paul's was a national undertaking, not merely a diocesan effort. The King honored his 1664 commitment of £1,000 to restore the old cathedral; in fact, he doubled it. Archbishop Sheldon, Bishop Henchman, and the Bishops of Durham and Winchester made significant contributions, but the other bishops didn't contribute to the building fund. Wren personally contributed to the fund.

On May 14, 1675, the King authorized the commencement of work on the Cathedral. On June 21, the first stone was laid without any accompanying ceremony. Wren walked around the site and marked the key locations of the foundation. He asked one of the workmen to bring him a flat stone from the rubbish pile to use as the guide from which all other measurements would be made. The workman struggled bringing a stone to be used as a marker and was relieved to drop the heavy load at the location indicated by the Surveyor-General. Many of the workmen around Wren looked down and read the word "RESURGAM"—I shall rise again—carved on the old marker that their fellow worker had selected. Wren and the workmen considered this to be a good luck omen.

Many talented tradesmen contributed to the building of St.

Paul's, including Assistant Surveyor John Oliver, who supervised the workmen, purchased materials, and audited the accounts; Laurence Spenser, Clerk of the Works, who acted as the timekeeper and kept the account books; Master-Mason Thomas Strong, who was succeeded by his brother, Edward Strong; ironworker Master-Carvers Tijou, from France, and Thomas Robinson; Stone-carvers Francis Baird and Caius Gabriel Cibber; and Jonathon Maine, who did the wood carving in the library and in the chapels on the west side of the Cathedral. The two most well-known wood-carvers were Grinling Gibbons and Philip Wood.

Wren's friend, John Evelyn, met Grinling Gibbons at Gibbons's run-down thatched cottage near Sage's Court at Deptford. Gibbons was carving a crucifix of Tintoret that impressed Evelyn. Evelyn introduced Gibbons to Wren, who employed him as a wood-carver at St. Paul's for many years. Gibbons's wood carvings for the choir-stalls in the Cathedral provide an outstanding example of his craft.

The story of Philip Wood's hiring as a wood-carver at St. Paul's is an unusual one. Wood, who was too poor to afford to buy the necessary woodcarving tools, hung around the building site until he saw that woodcarving was about to start. He approached one of the overseers to ask if he could get a job as a wood-carver. The overseer thought that Wood looked like a farmer and told him that: "They had no use for barn and stable work here." Wood continued to hang around the site until "a gentleman approached with papers in his hand and talked to the work people. At last his eye falling on me, he asked a workman, 'What does that fellow do here? I will have no persons about unless they do business.'"

The workman addressed by Wren told him that the young man was looking for work as a wood-carver but had been told that there was no job for him. When Wren asked him what experience he had, he replied that he had carved pig troughs. The workman laughed heartily at the young man from the country. Wren told him that he should go home and prepare wood carvings of a sow and her piglets, since that was something with which he was familiar. The workman got another laugh out of the young man's discomfiture.

Wood went home in near despair and told his landlady about his experience. She cheered him up and told him that they would buy a good piece of pearwood to use in carving the pig family. He completed his task and returned to the building site the following week. Again the overseer turned him away, but Wood waited until the Surveyor-General appeared. Wren was accompanied by a group of people, and the overseer attempted to prevent Wood from approaching him.

Wood presented his wonderful carvings of the pigs to Wren, who looked at them closely. Mr. Addison, one of Wren's companions, asked Wood if he would sell the carvings. Wood agreed to sell them and was given ten guineas for his work. Wren apologized to Wood for his earlier treatment and told him that he would have work as a wood-carver at the Cathedral as long as there was wood carving to be done.

Work proceeded on the Cathedral despite differences of opinion between the Commissioners that required adjudication by Wren. Wren persevered in keeping the work on the Cathedral moving and in ensuring that the design was implemented according to his plan. Lack of funds was a chronic problem, particularly since construction was proceeding simultaneously on housing and on the other churches that had been destroyed by the Great Fire.

Biographer John Lindsey described the Cathedral:

> Wren's intention all along had been that the dome should be the central figure of the church both within and without. The choir, the nave, and the transepts he planned of exactly the same design, proportion, and ornamentation: thus, the arcade of three arches in the choir is the same as the arcade of three arches in the nave and that of one each in the transepts.
>
> The arcade of the choir is completed by the apse, that of the nave by the magnificent vestibule flanked north-west and south-west by the chapels of St. Dunstan and of St. Michael and St. George

while the the arcade of each transept ends in a flat ornamental wall with a semi-circular porch outside. Each "arm" of the church is attached to the dome by walls and vast panels supporting a barrel arch of identical pattern while a similar arch joins the choir to the apse.

Wren was influenced by many sources in his design of St. Paul's. The dome displays the influence of Bramante's unexecuted design for St. Peter's Basilica in Rome, and the ribbed section of the dome reflects the work of Michelangelo. The Corinthian portico is similar to earlier Inigo Jones designs, and the execution of the dome design over eight arches was probably influenced by an unused Mansart plan. The overall plan for a Greek cross building may have come from a drawing of Webb's "ideal" churches. These influences take nothing away from Wren's overall effort. St. Paul's is a magnificent design with great proportion that displays considerable originality on the part of the architect.

St. Paul's Cathedral was under construction for thirty-five years, and the chief architect lived to see it completed. Wren persevered in confronting many obstacles, including the initial controversy of whether the Cathedral should be in the shape of a Greek cross or a Latin cross, the placement of the organ and its accompanying screen that would have limited the space for worship to 400 people, and struggling with the Commissioners about having Sir James Thornhill paint images of the life of St. Paul on the inside of the dome instead of using bright mosaics.

Furthermore, the chief architect was nagged continually that the work on the Cathedral was proceeding too slowly. In his *Annals*, Dean Milman noted that:

> A clause had crept into an Act of Parliament that, until the work should be finished, half his salary should be withheld from the Surveyor. The Commissioners proceeded to carry this hard clause into effect. This was not only a hardship, but a tacit

imputation that the Architect was delaying the completion of the work for his own emolument. It is indeed stated plainly in one of the Commissioner's papers that Sir Christopher, or someone employed by him, who, by many affidavits, have proved guilty of great corruption, may be supposed to have found their advantage to this delay....

In the matter of corruption and embezzlement the Commissioners, apart from suggesting that Wren himself had been responsible for the delay, concentrated their attacks on the workmen, notably the Master Carpenter, Jennings. Him they accused of selling quantities of material which had been charged to Cathedral accounts and, by pocketing the proceeds, making an income of fifteen hundred a year out of his deals. It is noteworthy that they were unable to produce any witnesses to these alleged illegal transactions, nor were they ever able to produce evidence that Jennings's accounts showed that he received anything more than his official salary.

Wren's son Christopher in his book, *Parentalia*, claims that his father laid the last stone for the Cathedral in 1710. In late 1711, Parliament declared that work had been completed and made the final payments on Wren's salary that had been held in arrears. Wren stayed on as Surveyor-General until he was eighty-four years old and had been employed on the old and the new St. Paul's for over fifty years. Despite his long-term courage in doing his job,,the final insult to him occurred in 1718, when his appointment was terminated, and he was replaced by a political appointee with no knowledge of architecture who lasted only a year as Surveyor-General.

Biographer John Lindsey puts Wren's achievement in designing and constructing St. Paul's into perspective:

The quality of St. Paul's, with its triumphs and its compromises, can be understood only if all the limiting conditions are remembered. Wren was building, in the age of late Baroque, for a Protestant community, and a conservative clergy, who wished to preserve the Latin cross plan which they had inherited from the Middle Ages. Money was short, materials came in slowly and, at the beginning at least, Wren lacked experience as an architect. He gained it by ceaselessly adapting himself to circumstances and using his mathematical genius to overcome difficulties.... Wren's triumph lies in his conquest of circumstances; and surely by any standards the design for the dome is great architecture. His own generation had no doubt about his quality. To them, the man had matched the moment.

Wren died on February 25, 1723. He was buried in the crypt under the choir at St. Paul's "with Great funeral State and Solemnity." Initially, his grave was marked by an unadorned black slab of marble with the inscription in Latin, "Under this stone lieth the Founder of this Church and City, Christopher Wren, who lived more than ninety years not for himself but for the public good." His son had a Latin inscription placed on the wall over his grave that ends with "Lector si monumentum requiris circumspice." (Reader, if you seek his monument, look around you.) He couldn't have chosen a more suitable epitaph.

THOMAS GARRETT (1789-1871) Underground Railroad Leader in Delaware

"Courage consists of equality to the problem before us."

Emerson, *Society and Solitudes: Courage*

Thomas Garrett, who helped over 2,900 slaves escape to the North, was highly regarded by his peers. Abolitionist William Lloyd Garrison expressed his feelings upon Garrett's death in a letter to one of his sons: "In view of his ... singularly beneficent life, there is no cause for sorrow, but [I would like] to express the estimation in which I held him, as one of the best men who ever walked the earth, and one of the most beloved among my numerous friends and co-workers in the cause of the oppressed and downtrodden race, now happily rejoicing in their heavenly wrought deliverance."

Thomas Garrett, one of eleven children of Thomas and Sarah Price Garrett, was born in Upper Darby, Pennsylvania, on August 21, 1789. Thomas, Sr., operated mills and was a scythe- and tool-maker. Young Thomas worked in his father's businesses.

Garrett's motivation to spend a lifetime supporting antislavery causes began when he was twenty-four-years old and still living at home with his parents. He had returned home one day to find his mother and sisters distressed. Two men had come to the house and kidnapped an African-American woman who worked for the family. Garrett pursued their wagon, following marks made by a broken wheel. He tracked them to the Navy Yard and then to Kensington, where the men had stopped at a roadside tavern. He found the kidnapped woman in the kitchen of the tavern and returned with her to Upper Darby.

During the time he was pursuing the kidnappers and while riding home, Garrett thought about the wrongs of the slavery system. It was wrong that men thought that they had a right to enter a home and carry off a woman against her will. He made a resolution to aid oppressed slaves in any way that he could.

On October 14, 1813, Garrett married Mary Sharpless of Birmingham, Pennsylvania, and, in 1822, they moved to

Wilmington, Delaware, a thriving town with plenty of opportunity for an ambitious young man. Garrett opened an iron, steel, and coal business. He had early difficulties, which are described by James A. McGowan in *Station Master on the Underground Railroad*:

> A rival house ... in the iron business, sought to run him off the track by reducing the price of iron to cost, but Friend Thomas, nothing daunted, employed a man to take his place in the store, tied on his leather apron, took to his hammer and anvil and in the prosecution of the trade learned from his father prepared to support his family with his own hands as long as the run lasted. Thus, by the sweat of his brow, he foiled the purpose of his rival and laid the foundation of what after many reverses became one of the permanent business houses of the city.

Garrett had few close friends and was looked upon with suspicion; his house was under constant surveillance by the police, who realized that it was a station on the underground railroad. He was not bothered by this lack of popularity or by adverse opinion because he knew that the Lord approved of his activities. Garrett believed in doing his duty. He thought that a man's duty is shown to him and that duty, once recognized, was an obligation. His approach to life was summarized by Geoffrey Hubbard: "Every Quaker defines his position fully and clearly by his life."

Garrett had a powerful physique and considerable personal bravery. He had no fear of the proslavery supporters who attempted to bully him. An example of his fearlessness was his response to a supporter of slavery who told Garrett that if he ever came to his town, he would shoot him. Garrett responded, "Well, I think of going that way before long, and I will call upon thee." He called upon the man as he had promised. Garrett said, "How does thee do friend? Here I am, thee can shoot me if thee likes." He was not shot.

Men confronted Garrett flourishing pistols and bowie knives.

He pushed them aside and told them that only cowards resorted to such measures. On one occasion, two men were overheard planning to kill him:

> He was warned, but having a meeting to attend that night, he went out as usual. In the street two men leaped upon him, but his brawny hands caught them by the backs of their necks and brought them up standing. He shook them well and looked them over, then said, "I think you look hungry. Come in and I will give you supper." He forced them into his house and his wife prepared a warm supper, while Friend Thomas chaffed them about their adventure, and turned the enmity into friendship.

On another occasion, he boarded a train in Wilmington to prevent an African-American woman from being carried off to the deep South. Several southerners attempted unsuccessfully to throw him off the train. At one point, a reward of $10,000 was offered for him in Maryland. He wrote to the parties offering the reward and told them that this was not enough. For $20,000, he would turn himself in.

On July 13, 1828, Garrett's wife, Mary, died. She had been his partner in underground railroad work. On January 7, 1830, he married Rachel Mendinhall, daughter of a Quaker merchant who was a director of the National Bank of Delaware & Brandywine. Perhaps due to her ill health, Rachel stayed in the background and was not as active a participant as Mary had been in antislavery activities.

In 1848, eight African Americans—a man, his wife, and six children—ran away from a plantation on the eastern shore of Maryland. Except for two of the children who had been born in slavery, they were free. They sought refuge at the home of a wealthy Quaker in Middletown, Delaware. Unfortunately, they had been followed. They were arrested and sent to jail in New Castle. The Sheriff and his daughter, who opposed slavery, notified Garrett of their plight.

Garrett visited the jailed family in New Castle and returned to

Wilmington. The following day, he and U.S. Senator Wales presented Judge Boothe with a writ of *habeas corpus*. Judge Boothe decided that there was no evidence to hold them, and, in the absence of evidence, "the presumption was always in favor of freedom." He discharged them. Garrett said, "Here is this woman with a babe at her breast, and the child suffering from a white swelling on its leg; is there any impropriety in my getting a carriage and helping them over to Wilmington?" Judge Boothe responded, "Certainly not."

Six weeks later, the slaveholders filed a suit against Garrett in New Castle for helping fugitive slaves escape. The trial, presided over by Judge Hall and Chief Justice Taney in May 1848, lasted three days. Garrett's friends suspected that the jury had been stacked against him. He was convicted, and every dollar of his property was taken from him. He responded, "Now, Judge, I do not think that I have always done my duty, being fearful of losing what little I possessed; but now that you have relieved me, I will go home and put another story on my house, so that I can accommodate more of God's poor."

Garrett's friends helped him in his time of difficulty. He was almost sixty years old, but he made the addition to his house and increased his support of escaped slaves. His activities were aided by donations from friends in England. He continued to work to help the slaves until President Abraham Lincoln freed them in 1863 by signing the Emancipation Proclamation.

Thomas Garrett died on January 25, 1871. During his lifetime, he had helped just under 3,000 slaves on their journey to the North. Not one of these slaves was captured on the road to freedom. The exception was a slave who escaped, lived in Canada for a number of years, and returned to Wilmington to preach. He was seized and returned to bondage.

Throughout his life, Garrett lived his principles: "I should have done violence to my convictions of duty, had I not made use of all the lawful means in my power to liberate those people, and assist them to become men and women, rather than leave them in the condition of chattels."

BRIGHAM YOUNG (1801-1877) Led the Mormons to the Salt Lake Valley

> When a furious mob murdered [Mormon founder Joseph] Smith, Young assumed the leadership of the Mormon survivors and redirected their vision toward new goals. Far beyond the Mississippi, in heretofore unsettled territory, lay the Great Basin to which he led the remnants of the Church and its followers. There Young supervised the building of a new society that soon attracted thousands of newcomers from other parts of the Union and from Europe as well.
>
> Oscar Handlin

Brigham Young, the sixth child and third son of John and Abigail Howe Young, was born on June 1, 1801, in Whitingham, Vermont. John Young was a farmer who moved frequently because of increasingly worn-out soil. Abigail Young was a relative of Elias Howe, one of the inventors of the sewing machine, and Samuel Gridley Howe, an eminent nineteenth-century reformer. She suffered from tuberculosis and had difficulty caring for the children and doing the chores around the house.

In 1802, John Young moved the family to Smyrna, New York. John cleared land for farming and built a log dwelling in an area known as Dark Hollow. The family's next move was to Genoa, east of Cayuga Lake. Brigham was introduced to hard work at an early age, including logging and driving a team of horses. The family was poor and hired Brigham out to neighbors to earn additional income. He attended the Drake School House and was tutored by his mother.

The Youngs were Methodists who originally had been New England Congregationalists. In Brigham's opinion, his parents were "the most strict religionists that lived upon the earth." The children were not allowed to use words such as "devil" and "I vow." Brigham held back from joining the Methodist church or any other church. He said a prayer to himself: "Lord, preserve me until I am old enough to have sound judgment, and a discreet mind ripened on a good, solid foundation of common sense."

Abigail Young died on June 11, 1815, just after Brigham's fourteenth birthday. He had been close to his mother; in his words, "Of my mother—she that bore me—I can say no better woman lived in the world." His older sister, Fanny, who had helped care for him as a child, returned home and became the stabilizing influence in the family. Brigham developed into an independent individual with a deliberate manner.

In 1815, the family moved again—to the Sugar Hill area near Tyrone. Their farm had many maple trees, and they went into maple sugar-making to supplement their income. Maple sugar could be bartered for flour and other necessities. In 1817, John Young married Hannah Dennis Brown, a widow with several children of her own. He broke up his household and moved in with his new wife. Sixteen-year-old Brigham's father told him: "You now have your time; go and provide for yourself."

Young moved to Auburn, where he became an apprentice to learn the trades of carpentry, glazing, and painting. An early project was the finish carpentry and painting of the new home of Judge Elijah Miller, the father-in-law of William H. Seward, a future Governor, U.S. Senator, and Secretary of State. The Seward Mansion, which Seward inherited from Judge Miller, has an ornate fireplace mantel crafted by Young. Young also worked on the construction of the Auburn Theological Seminary.

In 1823, Young moved to Port Byron, a fast-growing town on the new Erie Canal. He worked in a furniture repair shop, a wool carding mill, a pail factory, and a boatyard. One of his employers observed that he "would do more work in a given time and secure more and better work from his help without trouble than any man they have ever employed." In 1824, Young joined the Methodist church. He insisted on being baptized by immersion, although that was not the usual Methodist practice at the time.

On October 5, 1824, Young married Miriam Works, a beautiful blonde whom he had met while working at the pail factory. Their daughter, Elizabeth, was born in Port Byron. In 1828, the family moved to Oswego, where he worked on the construction of a large tannery. When the tannery was finished the following year, he moved his family to Mendon, where his father and several of his sisters had settled. Young built a house in Mendon and constructed a large undershot waterwheel on the creek that flowed through his property; it provided power for grindstones, lathes, and saws.

In June 1830, their second daughter, Vilate, was born. The childbirth temporarily incapacitated Miriam, who suffered with tuberculosis—the same ailment that had afflicted her mother-in-law. Young took part-time jobs so he could do more of the household chores while Miriam was bedridden. The family remained poor and contracted small debts.

While living in Port Byron, Young heard "rumors of a new revelation, to the effect of a new Bible written upon golden plates ... at Palmyra. I was somewhat acquainted with the coming forth of the Book of Mormon ... through ... the newspapers [and] many stories and reports ... circulated ... as the Book of Mormon was printed and ... scattered abroad." In June 1830, Young saw a copy of the Book of Mormon when Samuel Smith, a brother of Joseph Smith who had found the golden plates on Hill Cumorah, visited Mendon to preach about Mormonism and to sell copies of the "golden Bible."

In January 1830, Young, his brother, Phineas, and his good friend and neighbor, Heber Kimball, traveled to Columbia, Pennsylvania, the location of the nearest Mormon church, to observe Mormons interpreting their religion, prophesying, and speaking in tongues. Young returned to Mendon and then visited his brother, Joseph, a Methodist minister in Canada, to ask his opinion of the new religion. In early April, John, Sr., Joseph, and Phineas were baptized into the Mormon religion.

On April 14, Young was baptized by Elder Eleazer Miller in the stream behind his home. He said that before his clothes "were dry on my back [Elder Miller] laid his hands on me and ordained me an Elder, at which I marveled. According to the words of the Savior, I felt a humble, childlike spirit, witnessing unto me that my sins were forgiven." Ordination as an Elder gave Young the authority to preach the gospel. The rest of the family followed him in joining the new religion.

Four things that Young liked about Mormonism were its similarities to Puritanism, with its emphasis on common sense; its espousal of "Christian Primitivism," the restoration of Christianity as it existed at the time of Jesus Christ; its authoritarianism, which required unquestioning loyalty to the Mormon prophet Joseph Smith; and its lay priesthood, which provided a path to status and influence.

On September 8, 1832, Miriam Young died of tuberculosis. Young and his two daughters moved in with his friend, Heber Kimball. That fall, Young and Kimball traveled to the main Mormon settlement in Kirtland, Ohio, just east of Cleveland, to meet Joseph Smith—founder of the Church of Jesus Christ of Latter-Day Saints. Upon meeting the charismatic Mormon prophet, Young spoke in tongues and asked the Latter-Day Saints leader's opinion of his gift of tongues. Smith "told them that it was of the pure Adamic language.... It is of God, and the time will come when Brother Brigham Young will preside over this church."

Young returned to Mendon to preach Mormonism and traveled around upstate New York and Canada baptizing converts. In September 1833, he moved to Kirtland to be near Joseph Smith and the center of Mormon activity. He courted Mary Ann Angell, a former Baptist from Seneca, New York. In February 1834, Young and Mary Ann were married by Sidney Rigdon, an influential Mormon leader. Early the following year, Smith appointed Young one of the Council of Twelve Apostles, modeled on the Apostles of the New Testament, who were responsible for overseeing Mormon churches and missionary activity.

From 1835 through 1837, Young traveled around upstate New York, New England, and Canada spreading the word of Mormonism. On a return visit to Kirtland during this time, he supervised the completion of the Kirtland Temple. Smith encountered difficulties in Kirtland when he attempted to establish his own bank. Because of his indebtedness and his plan to print his own money, Smith was denied a state banking charter. He established the bank anyway; unfortunately, it was adversely affected by the Panic of 1837.

In 1838, Young was drawn into the conflict between Mormons and non-Mormons in Missouri. Non-Mormons were concerned about the Mormons' economic and political control of the region. A series of armed clashes began in Gallatin, Missouri, when non-Mormons attempted to prevent Mormons from voting. Three Mormons were killed at Crooked River, Caldwell County, and seventeen Mormons were killed and fifteen wounded seriously at Haun's Mill, Caldwell County, by a mob of over 200 men.

The Governor of Missouri, Lilburn Boggs, called out the Missouri militia and issued the order that Mormons "must be exterminated or driven from Missouri, if necessary, for the public good." Joseph Smith turned himself in to the authorities and his brother, Hyrum, and Sidney Rigdon were arrested. Young was the only senior member of the Council of the Twelve Apostles who was not in captivity. He appealed to the Missouri Legislature for compensation for Mormon property that had been seized. The Mormons received a token payment and, due to threats to their lives, left Missouri for Illinois.

In 1839, Young made his last visit to upstate New York while en route to a successful mission that more than doubled church membership in England. He promoted the increase in the number of English Elders and the immigration of English Mormons to the United States. During the next six years, over 4,000 Mormons immigrated to the United States from Great Britain. He also established a Mormon periodical, the *Millennial Star,* in England. Young clearly established a reputation as an efficient administrator and organizer.

Smith escaped from his six-month captivity and established the center of Mormon faith in Nauvoo, Illinois. In July 1841, when Young returned to Nauvoo, he found that it had become a rapidly growing city of 3,000; it would expand to 10,000 by the end of 1841. The Nauvoo Charter gave Mormons comprehensive powers of self-government, although they could not pass any laws contrary to the Illinois and U.S. Constitutions. The Mayor and city council formed their own municipal court, and the city controlled its own militia, the Nauvoo Legion.

Young was elected to the Nauvoo city council and was appointed editor of the Nauvoo newspaper, *The Times and Seasons*. His commitment to Mormonism was severely tested in 1841, when Joseph Smith endorsed the practice of polygamy for the Latter-Day Saints. Smith may have been influenced by the practices of the Oneida Community in New York State when he supported the concept of plural marriage. Initially, Young was appalled by the practice. He said that it "was the first time in my life that I had desired the grave." When he expressed his views to Smith, he was told, "Brother Brigham, the Lord will reveal it to you."

Young was faced with the dilemma of either practicing polygamy or defying the prophet Joseph Smith. Eventually, he accepted plural marriage. In June 1842, he married 20-year-old Lucy Ann Decker Seeley. On November 2, 1843, he married Augusta Ann Adams and Harriet Cook. In May 1844, he took his fourth plural wife, Clarissa Decker, the sister of his first plural wife. His wives lived in their own houses.

The practice of polygamy was the greatest source of difficulty for the Mormons, both within and outside of the church. Nauvoo was envied as the most prosperous city in Illinois, but its self-government was not easily accepted by non-Mormons. Smith realized that he must look to the Far West as "a place of refuge" where "the devil cannot dig us out." In February 1844, Smith asked the Council of Twelve to send a delegation westward toward California and Oregon to build a temple and to establish a government of their own.

The delegation to the West was delayed by Smith's decision to run for the Presidency of the U.S. in 1844 as an independent candidate. Young and other Mormon leaders did much of the campaigning for the candidate. Smith had problems of his own back in Nauvoo, however. A group of dissidents led by William Law split off from the Latter-Day Saints due to disagreements with Smith's policies, particularly polygamy. Law and his associates established a competing newspaper, the Nauvoo *Expositor*. Smith asked the city council to destroy the press and all copies of the newspaper, a blatant violation of freedom of the press.

Anti-Mormon feeling intensified around Nauvoo, and Smith, his brother, Hyrum, and two other Mormon leaders gave themselves up to county authorities in Carthage. On June 27, 1844, a large, organized mob entered the jail at Carthage and killed Smith and his brother, and wounded another of the Mormon leaders. Young, who was campaigning for Smith in Massachusetts at the time, courageously returned to Nauvoo by a roundabout route to avoid assassination.

Young's only serious rival for the Mormon presidency was Sidney Rigdon. Young's forceful speech, his alignment with the Council of Twelve, and his confidence that the Church would make the right decision made him the clear choice. Although Smith's brother, William, supported Young's election to the presidency, later he attempted to replace him. Anti-Mormon sentiment continued to run high, and Illinois Governor Thomas Ford repealed the Nauvoo charter, which disfranchised both the city police and the Nauvoo Legion. Earlier, he had ordered the Nauvoo Legion to return their state-supplied weapons.

In late 1844 and early 1845, Young married fifteen additional wives, five of whom had been plural wives of Joseph Smith. Only five of these wives bore offspring. It was thought that Young merely provided many of them with financial aid and the protection of his name. He had a strictly platonic relationship with one wife, Eliza R. Snow, who founded the Mormon Relief Society and was known as the church's "First Lady of Letters."

Illinois justice was unable to convict the killers of Joseph Smith and his brother, and anti-Mormon mobs burned barns and crops on farms around Nauvoo. Young realized that they would have to abandon Nauvoo and settle in a frontier sanctuary. Texas was considered a possible site, as were California, Oregon, and the Island of Vancouver. Young ruled out the latter two because they were involved in ongoing boundary disputes between the United States and Great Britain. He favored the Great Basin of Utah because it was remote and virtually uninhabited by whites.

In February 1846, the main body of Mormon settlers left Nauvoo. Young organized twenty-four companies of 100 each and personally selected the leader of each company. Mormons sold most of their property for a fraction of its value. Utopian Robert Owen and the Catholic Church looked at the property, particularly the Temple, but decided not to purchase it. Before leaving Nauvoo, Young was continually threatened with arrest. The Mormons' trek to the West was the largest and best-organized of all migrations.

They spent the first winter on Potawatomi Indian lands just north of Omaha, Nebraska. Young supervised the building of 538 log houses and 83 sod houses for 3,483 people. In early 1847, he assumed personal responsibility for the pilot company of 159 pioneers, seventy-two wagons, sixty-six oxen, and ninety-two horses. The company, whose goal was to chart the path to the Great Salt Lake Valley for others to follow, used artificial horizons, a circle of reflection, and sextants. They did not employ professional guides.

Initially, they traveled the Oregon Trail along the Platt River. They averaged ten miles a day. Dry buffalo dung was used as fuel for their fires. On the trail, they encountered hostile Pawnees and friendly Sioux Indians. On July 7, 1847, they reached Fort Bridger on the Green River. John C. Fremont's description of the Great Salt Lake Region was favorable; however, Jim Bridger, the famous scout, told them that the Indians in the area were unfriendly, and that the area's cold nights would prevent the growth of crops. When they got within fifty miles of the Great Salt Lake (near Ogden, Utah), another scout gave them a favorable report of their destination, including its agricultural potential.

On July 24, 1847, Young saw the Great Salt Lake Valley for the first time, from the mouth of Emigration Canyon, and said, "This is the place." Compared with Nauvoo, the Salt Lake Valley was dry and remote. It was forty miles long from north to south and twenty-five miles wide and bounded by majestic snow-capped mountains. Young laid out the city with streets eight rods wide in a perfect grid.

During the winter of 1847-48, Young reorganized the First Presidency of the Church and appointed Heber Kimball First

Counselor and his own cousin, Willard Richards, Second Counselor. Also, he assumed the designation of prophet, seer, and revelator that had been held by Joseph Smith. By the spring of 1848, the settlement had grown from 300 to over 5,000 people.

The first crop was severely reduced by an invasion of crickets, which they could not get rid of. Their prayers were answered when seagulls came from the Great Salt Lake to consume them. Mormons benefited economically during 1849, when wagonloads of gold prospectors passed through on their way to California. Mormons repaired the travelers' harnesses and wagons and sold supplies to them.

During 1849 and 1850, Young sought statehood for Utah and sent two representatives to Washington, D.C., to lobby for it. He did not want territorial status because it would involve federal observers that could limit his control. President Taylor denied the request for statehood; however, upon Taylor's death, President Fillmore granted territorial status to Utah, which was named for the Ute Indians in the region. Mormons had named it Deseret. Young was chosen as Utah's first Territorial Governor, and Mormons were appointed as Associate Justice of the Territory's Supreme Court, U.S. Marshal, and U.S. Attorney.

Young counseled keeping on friendly terms with the Ute Indians in the area. He asked Mormons to "feed them and clothe them ... never turn them away hungry" and "teach them the art of husbandry." In his opinion, "It was cheaper to feed the Indians than to fight them." From 1850 to 1855, the number of Mormons in the Salt Lake Basin grew from 5,000 to 60,000, mainly from the East but including 15,000 from Great Britain.

In May 1857, President Buchanan sent 2,500 federal troops to Utah to remove Young as Territorial Governor. As had occurred earlier, anti-Mormon sentiment was rampant, principally due to their practice of polygamy. The original commander of federal troops was replaced by Colonel Albert Sidney Johnston, who later distinguished himself as a Confederate General during the Civil War. The winter weather caused hardship for Colonel Johnston's contingent. As a goodwill gesture, Young sent 800 pounds of salt to

Johnston, who responded that he would "accept no favors from traitors and rebels."

Young accepted President Buchanan's appointed Governor, Alfred Cumming, but refused to let Colonel Johnston's men enter Salt Lake City. Young threatened to burn every structure built by the Mormons if the army entered the city. The Mormons vacated the city until July 1858, when peace was made with the federal government.

The settlement continued to expand. Young was a good businessman and by the late 1850s had an accumulated wealth between $200,000 and $250,000, earned from lumbering, lumber mills, real estate, and a tannery. He married more plural wives until, ultimately, he had fifty-five, with whom he had fifty-seven children.

On August 23, 1877, Young became very ill and was diagnosed with cholera. His condition worsened, and he died on August 27 exclaiming "Joseph! Joseph! Joseph!" John Taylor, senior member of the Council of Twelve, became President of the Church in 1880.

Brigham Young provided leadership for the Mormon Church at a critical period in its history, enabling it to become the largest religion founded in the United States. Also, he contributed heavily to the growth of the American frontier and is considered one of the great colonizers in the history of the United States.

ROALD AMUNDSEN (1872-1928) Discoverer of the South Pole

"Resolution . . . is omnipotent. He that resolves upon any great, and at the same time, good [objective], by that very resolution, has scaled the chief barrier to it. He will find it removing difficulties, searching out or making means, giving courage for despondency, and strength for weakness; and like the star in the East, to the wise men of old, ever guiding him nearer and nearer to the sum of all perfection."

T. Edwards

The life of Roald Amundsen is a notable example not only of determination in achieving personal goals but also of courage. From his youth, Amundsen planned a career as an explorer. To please his mother, he enrolled in medical school but dropped out when she died.

Amundsen was driven to explore the world to the exclusion of everything else, including marriage. He set his long-term goals at the age of fifteen after reading of the exploits of Sir John Franklin, the British explorer who attempted to find the Northwest Passage. Amundsen never wavered from his goals and eventually discovered the South Pole and the Northwest Passage that Franklin lost his life trying to discover. Amundsen was the first person to visit both the North Pole and the South Pole.

Roald Amundsen, the youngest of four sons, was born on July 16, 1872, on a farm near Borge, Norway. During his first year, his parents moved to Oslo, then known as Christiania. He became familiar with skating, skiing, and snowshoeing at an early age as did all young Norwegians. Amundsen was fourteen when his father died.

As a teenager, Amundsen built himself up physically to prepare for demands that would be placed upon him later. He hiked and skied and was physically very active. He played soccer in secondary school, not because he liked the sport but as part of his conditioning program. He slept with his bedroom window wide open during the winter to condition himself to the cold, something rarely done in Olso winters. He spent most of his free time in outdoor activities.

When he graduated from secondary school, Amundsen enrolled at the University of Olso to prepare for his medical studies. When his mother passed away during his third year, he dropped out of college. In later years, he looked back with relief that he left the university to pursue enthusiastically his life's goals.

Soon after dropping out of college, Amundsen was called up for compulsory military service. He welcomed it because he considered it his duty to serve and it afforded him an opportunity for additional physical training. Army medical doctors were amazed by his muscle development and his physique. They were so impressed with his physical development that they neglected to examine his eyes thoroughly. If they had, his farsightedness would have caused him to fail the examination..

Amundsen trained hard and enjoyed his army service, and was encouraged to make the army his career. At the age of twenty-two, he decided that he needed a challenge of his physical endurance. He convinced a friend, Leif Bjornsen, to undertake a winter trek that had not been accomplished before.

A forbidding plateau called the Hardangervidda lies west of Oslo. The plateau is 6,000 feet above sea level and extends over seventy-five miles toward the west coast of Norway in the direction of Bergen. Lapps pastured herds of reindeer on the central plateau during the warmer months of the year, but they left during the winter. They had built a few crude huts to use in the cold, rainy periods of autumn.

Mogen farm was located near the eastern edge of the Hardangervidda, and Garen farm was near the western edge of the plateau. No one had ever crossed the plateau from one farm to the other. This presented Amundsen with precisely the challenge that he was seeking.

Amundsen and Bjornsen skied to Mogen on the first leg of their journey and stayed a week with an older couple while waiting for a storm to end. The family tried to persuade Roald and Leif to turn back because of the danger that they faced. As soon as the storm subsided, however, the friends began their journey across the plateau, traveling light because Amundsen estimated that they could reach Garen in two days. In addition to their skis and snowshoes, they carried only chocolate bars, crackers, an alcohol lamp, sleeping bags made from reindeer hide, a map, and a compass.

At the end of the first day they found one of the herders' huts. It had been boarded up, and the chimney was covered to keep out the snow. Leif injured his hand while removing boards to gain access to the hut. They made porridge from a sack of flour that they found there. They had to wait two days for the weather to clear enough to resume their trek. They found no hut at the end of the second day and had to sleep in the open. They stopped when it became too dark to see the crevasses.

Amundsen attempted to protect himself from the weather by digging a hole in the snow. When he awoke, he could not move and was having difficulty breathing. He was entombed by the wet snow that had fallen during the night and had turned to ice. He could hear Leif attempting to dig him out with a ski pole. It took several hours of hard work.

Amundsen discovered that the bags containing their food had disappeared, either sunken into slush and covered with ice or taken by a wild animal. They trudged onward until Amundsen realized that he was alone. Leif had fallen into a snow-covered crevasse about thirty feet deep. He was unhurt but could not climb out unaided. With difficulty, Amundsen pulled him out. They traveled four more days without food; area streams provided drinking water. Finally they reached a haystack from the previous growing season.

Leif was too tired to move the next morning, but Amundsen reconnoitered the area and found a set of ski tracks. He followed them until he caught up with the skier. They went back and woke up Leif and then went to the nearby farm, Mogen, the farm from which they had started. Later, the story unfolded. The farmer at Garen, at the western edge of the plateau, went looking for sheep that had strayed and found two pairs of ski tracks coming from the East and bending back around toward the East. He was astounded to see tracks at all, let alone tracks bending back upon themselves.

Amundsen and Leif had traversed twice a plateau that had not been traversed once previously. Amundsen learned three things from this outing:

• Ensure that the planning for the expedition is sound.
• Be well versed in the techniques of navigation.
• Do not take any unnecessary chances.

In 1894, Amundsen signed on as a deckhand on a sailing ship to learn seamanship and navigation. He sailed for three years and felt that he was ready to take the examination for Captain, but he did not have the necessary experience. In 1897, in Antwerp, Belgium, he signed on as first mate on the ship, *Belgica,* scheduled to sail to Antarctica as the Belgian Antarctic Expedition. The Captain was Adrien DeGerlache, a Belgian. Dr. Frederick Cook of Brooklyn, New York, the ship's doctor, was the only member of the ship's company with polar experience. He had sailed five years previously with Robert Peary on an expedition to Greenland.

On August 23, 1897, the *Belgica* sailed southward. The ship made numerous landings in Antarctica, and the crew did some of the early mapping of the continent. Captain DeGerlache was determined to sail as far south as he could. They found themselves 100 miles within the ice pack, encircled by ice, with no channels to the open sea. Since they had not planned on wintering over in the Antarctic, they did not have sufficient food or supplies. The only winter clothing they had on board was enough for a small shore party, not enough for the entire crew.

The crew suffered from scurvy, and eventually the Captain and the expedition commander were prostrated by it. Dr. Cook and Amundsen provided leadership for the crew, who initially refused to eat seal and penguin meat. Dr. Cook and Amundsen convinced them that their survival depended upon it. They were trapped in the ice for thirteen months until they broke through with the help of explosive charges.

Recording meteorological readings for an entire year was one of the achievements of the expedition. The readings served as a basis for the early climatology of the region. Another achievement was the advancement of the training and experience in polar exploration of Roald Amundsen.

Amundsen's next goal was to lead an expedition of his own. He passed his examination for a master's license and visited the well-known explorer, Dr. Fridjof Nansen, who warned him of a life of hardship and that the life of an explorer and marriage were not compatible. Amundsen told him that his goals were set and asked for a letter of reference to use in obtaining backers for an expedition. The letter helped in raising funds, obtaining supplies, and gaining technical support. Amundsen worked at two jobs to raise money.

In 1900, Amundsen made a down payment on a forty-seven-ton fishing boat that was twenty-seven years old, the same age as he was. The sloop *Gjoa* was sixty-nine-feet long with a beam of twenty-one and a half feet, carried 300 yards of canvas, and had an auxiliary gasoline engine. His critics thought that he needed a larger vessel for expeditions; however, he intended to push his small ship between the ice floes instead of breaking the ice with a larger ship.

Obtaining sufficient financial support was difficult, even with Dr. Nansen's letter. On June 15, 1903, Amundsen received a letter from the Bailiff that warned him of a potential lawsuit and seizure of his ship and supplies unless he paid his bills. He decided not to wait to see if the Bailiff was serious. That same night, Amundsen and his crew of six sailed from Oslo to find the Northwest Passage through over a hundred miles of land masses in the Canadian Arctic to Alaska. He was about to accomplish what Sir John Franklin failed to do in four attempts. Franklin perished on his last expedition of two ships, the *Erebus* and the *Terror,* along with 105 members of the crews, between 1845 and 1847. They were not found until 1854. Exploration was a hazardous occupation.

Guided by the writing of Sir Leopold McClintock, Amundsen chose a route south of the most obvious one due west from Boothia Peninsula. A shipboard fire broke out but was put out quickly. West of the peninsula, the *Gjoa* ran aground on a shoal, and many supplies had to be jettisoned to lighten the ship to refloat her. Coming off the shoal, the rudder was moved upward off its hinges, and Amundsen could not steer the ship. Fortunately, the rudder pins later fell back into place of their own accord.

The *Gjoa* and her crew collected meteorological information in the Canadian Arctic for two winters. They verified Ross's placement of the magnetic North Pole years previously and encountered two Eskimo villages that were friendly to them. On August 26, 1905, they sighted the American whaler, *Charles Hansen,* of San Francisco. Captain James McKenna of the *Charles Hansen* congratulated Amundsen on finding the Northwest Passage and told him that he and his crew planned to winter over near Hershel Island. The *Gjoa* wintered over there also, but Amundsen did not want to wait until spring to tell the world of his accomplishment. He went by dogsled to Eagle City, Alaska, site of the nearest telegraph station.

On October 19, the *Gjoa* arrived in San Francisco, where Amundsen and his crew were feted with a parade, a banquet, and receptions. The Norwegian Colony of San Francisco raised funds to buy the *Gjoa* and to donate her for exhibition in Golden Gate Park. Amundsen went on the lecture circuit describing his expedition and his visits with the Eskimo communities. He was invited to meet with President Theodore Roosevelt.

Amundsen earned enough money on the lecture tour to pay his debts in Norway. However, many of his creditors refused to accept payment; they were happy to have participated in a successful venture.

Amundsen prepared for his next expedition, to the North Pole. Dr. Nansen offered him a ship that he had designed for polar exploration; smooth, rounded sides reduced the possibility of being crushed by ice. The *Fram* was 119 feet long and had a beam of thirty-six feet. She was a much larger and more comfortable ship than the *Gjoa*. Amundsen planned to sail the *Fram* around to Alaska and then, using the drift theory espoused by Dr. Nansen, become frozen in the Arctic ice pack and drift to, or over, the North Pole.

However, while Amundsen was preparing for this expedition, word was received that Admiral Robert E. Peary had reached the North Pole by sledge on April 6, 1909. Amundsen was extremely disappointed, and many of his backers dropped out. He changed his plans but told no one of his new plans. Some of his backers wondered why he was proceeding to the North Pole after it had already been discovered. Others wondered why he was loading a thirteen-foot by twenty-six-foot prefabricated hut on the *Fram* if he planned to drift over the North Pole. Also, he loaded ninety-seven sled dogs and coal, which he could easily obtain in Alaska.

Amundsen realized that he could not hide his new plans for long. On September 10, 1910, after taking on supplies at Funchal, Madeira Islands, he announced to the crew that their destination was the Bay of Whales, Antarctica. He sent a telegram to Captain Robert Falcon Scott in Melbourne, Australia, who was also preparing an expedition to Antarctica: "Am going south—Amundsen."

Amundsen's expedition party landed at the Bay of Whales and set up the hut two miles from where the *Fram* was anchored. From this base camp, Amundsen's men established several supply depots along their route that crossed the Axel Heiberg Glacier and the Devil's Glacier. Three tons of food were stored for later consumption.

Scott's base camp was established at Cape Evans, 400 miles away. Unlike Amundsen, who was relying on Husky sled dogs for transportation, Scott was using Manchurian ponies and motorized sledges; he had developed a distrust for sled dogs on earlier expeditions. Scott's ship, *Terra Nova,* without Scott, who was establishing a string of supply depots along his route at the same time that Amundsen was establishing his, put in at the Bay of Whales while en route to King Edward VII Land. The two parties cautiously exchanged information; both were very much aware that they were in a race for the South Pole.

The *Fram* left for Buenos Aires, from which she started a transoceanic survey eastward to the west coast of Africa. She would return to the Bay of Whales the following summer to pick up the nine-member expedition. They had to wait until the Antarctic spring—autumn in the Northern Hemisphere—to arrive before they could begin their quest for the Pole. After a start aborted by consistent cold weather, Amundsen and four of his men set out for the Pole on October 19, 1911. Their food caches along their path were marked by flags mounted on twenty-foot-long bamboo poles.

Scott had to carry considerable food for his Manchurian ponies and fuel for his motorized sledges. Amundsen had more options than Scott; his dogs could be killed for food for other dogs and for members of the expedition, if necessary. In fact, the first option was used. Amundsen and his men had several accidents en route to the Pole, mainly when dogsleds broke through a thin crust or fell into a crevasse in poor visibility.

Amundsen's party planted a Norwegian flag when it reached the South Pole on December 14, 1911, and placed additional flags at the four compass points ten miles from the central flag. They began their return to their base camp on December 17 and arrived there on January 25.

The Scott expedition was less fortunate. It reached the flag and the tent left by Amundsen on January 18, 1912. All five men in the Scott party perished on the return trip to their base as determined by records found later. They died eleven miles from one of their food caches. At the end, they were on foot; the ponies and motorized sledges had failed them. One member of the Scott party, Petty Officer Evans, died of a head injury, and another member, Captain Lawrence Oates, walked away from the camp with no intent of returning when he began to slow the others down.

In November 1912, a search party found the corpses of the three remaining men in the party, Scott, Bowers, and Wilson, along with Scott's diary and some photographs. In his diary, Scott left the message "Had we lived, I should have had a tale to tell of the hardihood of my companions which would have stirred the heart of every Englishman. These rough notes and our bodies must tell the tale."

At Hobart, Tasmania, Amundsen went ashore to send a message to Norway that he had discovered the South Pole. However, the Royal Society of England responded, "We will wait to hear from Scott. His expedition was well equipped, while this adventurer who was supposed to have gone to the North Pole and claims to have wound up at the South Pole could not possibly have done it." Textbooks were printed in England that gave Scott credit for the discovery of the South Pole. When Scott's diary was found, he gave credit to Amundsen for his discovery. Amundsen was awarded honors by many governments and scientific societies, including the National Geographic Society in the United States.

Amundsen returned to Norway, where he invested in the shipbuilding business, made profitable by World War I. He had another ship built, the *Maud,* named for Norway's Queen. On July 15, 1918, he sailed along the Arctic coast of Russia to Alaska. This five-year voyage was only moderately successful. Toward the end of this trip, his business manager defrauded him, causing Amundsen to declare bankruptcy.

Amundsen returned to the United States to raise funds by lecturing to finance another expedition. He met American financier Lincoln Ellsworth, who offered to finance an expedition by seaplane to the North Pole and to share leadership with Amundsen. This unsuccessful expedition was followed by an expedition over the North Pole by dirigible. They dropped flags over the North Pole. Amundsen became the first person to visit both the North Pole and the South Pole, one by air and one by land.

Following this dirigible flight, Amundsen retired from exploring. However, another team crashed while attempting to fly over the North Pole in a dirigible. Amundsen was asked to help the rescue party. His aircraft developed engine trouble shortly after taking off from Spitzbergen and crashed into the sea, killing all on board.

Amundsen's wish was, "When death comes to me, may it do so while I'm busy at my life's work, while I'm doing something good and useful." On the maps of the world, Amundsen Glacier, Amundsen Gulf near the Beaufort Sea in the Arctic, and Amundsen Sea off the Walgreen Coast in the Antarctic mark the explorer's accomplishments.

CHAPTER 4

ACHIEVERS / ACTIVISTS

"Presence of mind and courage in distress are more than
armies to procure success."

John Dryden, *Aureng-Zebe*

HARRIET TUBMAN (1820-1913) Conductor on the Underground Railroad

"When I found I had crossed that [Mason-Dixon] line, I looked at my hands to see if I was the same person. There was such glory over everything; the sun came like gold through the trees, and over the fields, and I felt like I was in heaven."

Harriet Tubman

William Still, Philadelphia abolitionist leader, commented on Harriet Tubman's role in the underground railroad:

> Her success was wonderful. Time and time again she made successful visits to Maryland on the underground railroad, and would be absent for weeks at a time, running daily risks while making preparations for herself and passengers. Great fears were entertained for her safety, but she seemed wholly devoid of personal fear. The idea of being captured by slavehunters or slaveholders never seemed to enter her mind.

She was resolved to do her part to free those members of her race still in captivity.

Harriet Ross Tubman, one of eleven children of Harriet Greene and Benjamin Ross, was born in 1820 on a plantation in Dorchester County on the Eastern Shore of Maryland. The plantation on Big Buckwater River, which was owned by Edward Brodas, was 100 miles south of the Mason-Dixon Line and sixty miles from Baltimore. Harriet's parents were full-blooded Africans of the Ashanti, a West African warrior people.

Harriet, who was called Araminta at birth, was born in a slave cabin with an open fireplace and without windows or furniture. The family slept on a clay floor. When she was five years old, Harriet was hired out to a family named Cook. Mrs. Cook used Harriet to wind yarn.

Because she was slow at the job, Harriet was turned over to Mr. Cook, who put her to work tending his muskrat traps. She waded in the cold water of the river with a thin dress and no shoes and eventually developed bronchitis and a high fever. Mr. Cook thought she was faking illness and returned her to her home plantation, where she recovered from bronchitis and a case of measles.

Harriet was hired out again, this time as a baby nurse and housekeeper. She said, "I was so little that I had to sit on the floor and have the baby put in my lap. And that baby was always on my lap except when it was asleep or when its mother was feeding it." When the baby awakened during the night, Harriet was expected to rock it in its cradle to prevent it from crying. If the baby's crying awoke Mrs. Cook, she would beat Harriet with a cowhide whip that left permanent scars on her back and neck.

Harriet was fed scraps from the table and was hungry most of the time. When she was seven, she took a lump of sugar from the sugar bowl. Mrs. Cook saw her take it and got out her whip. Harriet fled the house and lived with pigs in the pigpen for five days, competing with them for potato peelings and other scraps of food. Finally, she returned to the Cook's home, where she was given a severe beating and sent home to the Brodas plantation.

Harriet was then hired out to split fence rails and load wagons with lumber. The heavy work was difficult for her, but she preferred it to being under the thumb of the mistress of the house. In her early teens, she worked as a field hand and saw many examples of cruelty to slaves on the plantation.

Later in life, she said of the owners and overseers, "They didn't know any better. It's the way they were brought up ... with the whip in their hand. Now it was not that way on all plantations. There were good masters and mistresses, as I have heard tell. But I did not happen to come across any of them."

In 1835, when she was fifteen years old, Harriet saw a slave sneak away from the plantation. The tall African American was followed by the overseer with his whip and by Harriet. The overseer soon caught the runaway slave and asked Harriet to hold the man while he tied him up. She refused. The black man ran away, and

Harriet stood in the way to prevent pursuit. The overseer picked up a two-pound weight and threw it at Harriet. It struck her in the middle of her forehead, fractured her skull, caused profuse bleeding, and gave her a severe concussion.

Harriet was in a coma for weeks. For the rest of her life, she was affected by severe headaches and "sleeping fits," during which she would fall asleep for a few minutes—sometimes in the middle of a conversation. She was left with a depression in her forehead and a disfiguring scar. While she was in bed recovering, her master brought prospective owners to her bedside in attempts to sell her. No one wanted to buy her, even at the lowest price; "They said I wasn't worth a penny."

When Harriet had regained her strength, she was hired out to John Stewart, a local contractor. Initially, she worked as a maid in Stewart's home, but she begged him to let her work outdoors with the men. She cut wood, drove a team of oxen, and plowed. Soon she was swinging an ax to cut timber for the Baltimore shipbuilding industry. When work was slack on the Stewart farm, she was allowed to hire herself out to cut and haul wood for neighboring farmers. For this privilege, she paid Stewart fifty dollars a year and was permitted to keep everything she earned above that amount. She put away a small nest egg from this work.

While Harriet toiled at heavy outdoor work, she dreamed of being free. She thought, "I had reasoned this out in my mind; there was one of two things I had a right to, liberty or death; if I could not have one, I would have the other. For no man would take me alive; I should fight for my liberty as long as my strength lasted, and when it came time for me to go, the Lord would let them take me."

In 1844, Harriet married John Tubman, a free African American who lived nearby. John Tubman had been born free because his parents had been freed when their master died. Her husband's freedom did not change Harriet's slave status. Furthermore, her children would belong to the plantation. The constant threat to slaves in Maryland was to be "sold South," that is, sold to plantation owners from Alabama, Georgia, Louisiana, or Mississippi, where conditions for slaves were much harsher than in states closer to the Mason-Dixon Line.

One day, Harriet heard that two of her sisters had been sold and were being transported south in chains. She knew of the underground railroad and of people who helped slaves escape. She did not know geography, but she knew enough to follow the North Star to freedom.

Harriet tried to convince three of her brothers to come with her, but they were afraid of being captured and punished. She knew that her husband did not want to travel to the North; in fact, he would have turned her in if he had known that she was leaving.

Tubman left the plantation in the middle of the night with a loaf of cornbread, some salt herring, and her prized possession—a patchwork quilt. As she left, she sang an old spiritual:

> I'll meet you in the morning,
> When I reach the promised land,
> On the other side of Jordan.
> For I'm bound for the promised land.

Tubman went to the house of a woman who was known to help slaves escape. The woman took her in and gave her a slip of paper noting her next stop on the way to freedom. Tubman was so grateful that she gave the woman her quilt. She was tired when she arrived at the next stop early in the morning. The woman opened the door and handed her a broom and told her to start sweeping the yard.

At first, Harriet was suspicious; then she realized that no one would question a slave working around the house. That evening, the woman's husband put her in his wagon, covered her with vegetables, and took her to the next stop, generally following the course of the Choptank River.

Tubman finally crossed the Mason-Dixon Line and entered Pennsylvania. She was free, but she did not have any contacts to help her find a job and a place to live. In her words, "I was a stranger in a strange land."

Tubman traveled to Philadelphia, where she found a job in a hotel kitchen cooking and washing dishes. She met two founders of the Philadelphia Vigilance Committee, James Miller McKim, a white clergyman, and William Still, a freeborn African American. They needed someone to guide a slave family north from Cambridge, Maryland. Harriet volunteered, but they hesitated letting her go because she might be retained in the South as a slave. When she heard that the family was her sister, Mary, and her brother-in-law, John Bowley, she insisted on going. She brought them to safety in Philadelphia.

In the spring of 1851, Tubman made her second trip south to guide fellow slaves northward. This time she guided her brother, James, and two of his friends to freedom. The overseer and the hounds were on their trail. Tubman evaded the dogs by crossing an ice-cold river. None of them could swim, and the men opposed the crossing. She waded out into swift-flowing water up to her chin to prove that they could make it across. If she had not changed their route on a hunch, they would have been captured.

On her next trip to Dorchester County, Maryland, Tubman stopped at her husband's cabin. She found that he had remarried and had no interest in traveling north. She brought several slaves back to Philadelphia, being very careful in country in which she was known.

Tubman traveled northward through Delaware, waiting until the last moment to cross into Maryland because Delaware was the site of the headwaters of many rivers that drained through the Eastern Shore into Chesapeake Bay. Also, the State's African-American population in 1860 contained only 1,798 slaves out of a total of 21,627. Delaware was the only southern state in which an African American was assumed to be free until proved to be a slave.

When she approached a stop on the underground railroad, Tubman hid her "passengers" before she rapped on the door. Then she would announce that she was "a friend with friends." Many of her trips north were through Wilmington, Delaware, the home of Thomas Garrett, a leader of the underground railroad movement.

On September 18, 1850, the passage of the Fugitive Slave Act made helping escaped slaves riskier. U.S. Marshals were empowered to catch runaways and return them to their owners. Anyone assisting a fugitive could be fined $1,000 and sent to jail. Slavecatchers were hired to pursue runaway slaves who had thought that they were safe in the North.

More slaves were now going to Canada, which was beyond the reach of the Fugitive Slave Act and the slavecatchers. Tubman said, "I wouldn't trust Uncle Sam with my people no longer." Eventually, she moved from Philadelphia to St. Catharines, Ontario, where she lived for five years.

In December 1851, Tubman made her fourth trip south. On her return, she guided another of her brothers and his wife to freedom. When she reached Garrett's home in Wilmington, she added nine more passengers, including a baby. From this trip onward, she carried a sedative to keep baby passengers quiet.

Between 1851 and 1857, Tubman made a spring trip and a fall trip to Maryland's Eastern Shore each year. On these trips, she met many of the leaders of the underground railroad movement, including John Brown, Frederick Douglass, J. W. Loguen, and Gerrit Smith. Brown called Tubman "General Tubman."

On one of her trips, Tubman had a nervous passenger who panicked and wanted to turn back. She knew that if he were captured, he would be tortured to describe escape methods and "stations" on the road north. She pointed a gun at his head and told him to keep walking, while reminding him that if he were dead he could not reveal any information. This occurred more than once on her trips on the underground railroad. Tubman frequently stopped at Cooper House in Camden, Delaware, and hid her passengers in a secret room above the kitchen. In Odessa, Delaware, they hid in a concealed loft over the sanctuary in a Quaker meeting house.

On many farms, slaves hid in a "potato hole," a rough vegetable cellar. On one occasion, Tubman pretended to be reading a book when the slavecatchers passed by. One of the men said to the other, "This can't be the woman. The one we want can't read or write."

People began to call Tubman "the Moses of her people." A $12,000 reward was offered for her capture. She made her last journey on the underground railroad in 1860. In nineteen trips, she led over 300 slaves to their freedom.

During the Civil War, Tubman worked with slaves who had been left behind when their owners joined the Confederate Army. Major General David Hunter was pleased to have her help with the slaves at Beaufort, South Carolina. She also served as a nurse at Hilton Head, South Carolina, and in Florida. For three years of service to the federal government, she was paid only $200, most of which was spent to build a washhouse where she instructed slave women in doing laundry to support themselves.

During the summer of 1863, Tubman worked as a scout for Colonel James Montgomery, who commanded an African-American regiment. Harriet assembled a network of spies, who notified her which slaves were ready to leave their master and serve in the Union Army. She was supposed to receive a reward for recruiting slaves to the Grand Army of the Republic. She was owed at least $1,800 for her efforts, but she was never paid.

In 1864, Tubman was exhausted, and her seizures were occurring more frequently. She went to Auburn, New York, to rest and recuperate. In 1867, Harriet's friend, Sarah Bradford, wrote a biography about her and turned over the proceeds of the book, $1,200, to her. Some of the money went to African Americans who needed food and clothing.

While living in Auburn, she heard that her husband, John Tubman, had died. On March 18, 1869, Tubman married Nelson Davis, whom she had met in South Carolina during the war. William H. Seward, Secretary of State in the Lincoln and Andrew Johnson administrations, attended her wedding. Seward had obtained property for Tubman when she first moved to Auburn; they maintained their friendship until he died in 1872.

In 1888, Tubman purchased a 25-acre property at a public auction to establish a home for African Americans who were ill and needy. She lacked the money to build the home, so she deeded the property to the African Methodist Episcopal Zion Church. The church built the home, but Tubman was unhappy when she heard that it cost $100 to enter it.

Tubman's second husband died in 1888. In 1890, Congress approved pensions for widows of Civil War veterans. Since Davis had served in the Union Army, she was entitled to eight dollars a month, which was increased to twenty dollars a month in 1899. Except for $200, this was the only money she received from the government; she was never fully paid for her efforts during the Civil War.

On March 10, 1913, Tubman died of pneumonia at the age of ninety-three, after living two years in the home that she had helped to establish. The Auburn post of the Grand Army of the Republic gave her a military funeral at which Booker T. Washington spoke.

Tubman was truly the Moses of her people; she was also an abolitionist, a humanitarian, a nurse, and a spy. Today, she is mainly remembered for her underground railroad activities, about which she said, "I never ran my train off the track, and I never lost a passenger."

CLARA BARTON (1821-1912) Founder of the American Red Cross

"A tremendous humanitarian . . . she nevertheless defied the usual way of doing things when it presented obstacles instead of solutions. She brought to her work not only a rare gift for organization but a persistence and determination that could overcome any obstacle in her path. The life of a person with vision is often one of struggle, of constantly fighting the status quo. Barton's life was filled with her battles for progress. She was one of the first . . . to realize that nursing must be done at the battlefront and that female nurses could be employed to do it. She was one of the first in her country to comprehend the importance of having the Red Cross in the United States. . . . She may have been the first person to realize the the International Red Cross could be used to aid people in times of peace."

Leni Hamilton, *Clara Barton*

Clara Barton, founder of the American Red Cross, was the youngest of five children. Clara's favorite brother was David. In July 1832, she saw David fall feet-first from the ridge post of a barn onto a pile of timber in the cellar. He developed a chronic headache, and, as the summer progressed, he contracted a fever.

Ten-year-old Clara became her brother's nurse. In her words, "From the first days and nights of his illness, I remained near his side. I could not be taken away from him, except by compulsion, and he was unhappy until my return. I learned to take all the directions for his medicines from his physicians . . . and to administer them like a genuine nurse. . . . thus it came about that I was the accepted and acknowledged nurse of a man almost too ill to recover."

Two doctors told the Bartons that their son's condition was hopeless. Clara cheered him up, fed him, bathed him, and read to him. She rarely left his side for two years. Finally, a new doctor, who was a believer in "hydrotherapy," examined David. He moved the young man to his sanatorium and began water therapy. David returned home in three weeks and was fully recovered in six weeks. He owed his life to his little sister, who gave him constant care and the will to live long enough to be cured.

Barton had many relatives who were teachers, and, at the age of 17, she passed an oral examination and began to teach school. She was an excellent teacher and was known for her discipline. After teaching for 12 years, she enrolled at the Clinton Liberal Institute to further her education. Upon completion of the program, she accepted a teaching position in Bordentown, New Jersey.

At the outbreak of the Civil War, Barton volunteered to help at the Washington Infirmary. She heard that the 6th Massachusetts regiment from Worchester had been attacked by a mob of Confederate sympathizers while traveling through Baltimore. Four men were killed, dozens were wounded, and all their baggage was stolen. They were dressed in winter uniforms and woolen underwear unsuitable for the spring and summer weather in Washington.

Using her own money, Barton furnished the men with summer underwear, eating utensils, food, pots, and pans, as well as handkerchiefs, needles, soap, thread, and towels. She advertised in the *Worchester Spy*, their hometown newspaper, that she would receive and distribute provisions for area servicemen. She received so many items that she had to ask the army quartermaster to warehouse them.

Barton heard that little medical care had been provided to the wounded after the disastrous First Battle of Bull Run. The wounded weren't treated, and they were left without food and water. She offered her services as a nurse, but encountered resistance. In the 1860s, women weren't considered strong enough to deal with conditions at the front. Propriety was also an issue. Finally, she received the long-awaited permission from Dr. William Hammond, Surgeon General of the U. S.: "Miss C. H. Barton has permission to go upon the sick transports in any direction—for the purpose of distributing comforts for the sick and wounded—of nursing them, always subject to the direction of the surgeon in charge."

Barton was introduced to battlefield nursing at the Battle of Cedar Run in Virginia. She arrived with a wagon load of supplies just as brigade surgeon James Dunn was considering how to treat the wounded without supplies. He called her the "Angel of the Battlefield," a name that stayed with her. Her second battlefield service was treating the staggering casualties of the Second Battle of Bull Run in August 1862.

At the Battle of Chantilly, Barton had three sleepless nights in a row; she slept for two hours on the fourth night lying in water from the heavy rains. Returning to Washington, the train carrying the wounded was almost captured by the Confederate cavalry, who burned the station from which they had just departed.

At Antietam, when Barton arrived with supplies that were vitally needed, brigade surgeon Dunn was using corn husks for bandages. While she was giving a drink of water to a wounded soldier, a bullet passed through her sleeve, and the soldier fell back dead. Another soldier asked her to use his pocket knife to remove a musket ball from his cheek; he couldn't wait for the surgeon. With a sergeant holding the soldier's head, she removed the ball. These are examples of Barton's hands-on empathy for her patients.

In 1864, Barton was Superintendent of Nurses for General Benjamin Butler's Army of the James. She organized hospitals and their staffs and supervised their administration. After the war, Barton collected information on soldiers who were missing in action. As with her nursing jobs, she worked without pay. She located over 22,000 missing soldiers; eventually, she was paid for her efforts. She went to Europe to rest and stayed with friends in Switzerland.

Dr. Louis Appia of the Red Cross visited Barton. He asked why the United States had rejected his offer three times to join the Red Cross. Barton had not heard of the organization founded by Jean-Henri Dunant. After witnessing the bloody Battle of Solferino with 40,000 casualties, Dunant wrote *A Memory of Solferino* in which he proposed the formation of an international relief organization. The Swiss-based organization chose for their symbol a red cross on a white background—the reverse of the color scheme of the Swiss flag. Clara was influenced by Dunant and began to consider forming a relief organization in the United States.

In 1873, Barton returned home. She spent the next four years convalescing from a nervous disorder that caused migraine headaches and periods of blindness. In March 1876, she moved to Dansville, New York, to improve her health at a sanatorium. After a year's rest with wholesome food in a peaceful environment, Barton completely regained her health.

While living in Dansville, Barton worked to bring the United States into the International Red Cross. She discovered that the reason for the resistance in the United States to joining the international organization was that it was considered a wartime relief organization. Barton pointed out the need for such an organization in addressing peacetime disasters, such as earthquakes and floods. She went to Washington, D.C., to convince President Garfield's cabinet of the importance of a U.S. role in the international relief organization.

When Barton returned to Dansville, the townspeople asked her to help form a local chapter of the Red Cross. On August 22, 1881, the first American chapter of the Red Cross was established in Dansville. The first disaster addressed by the chapter was a Michigan forest fire that took 500 lives and destroyed 1,500 homes. On March 16, 1882, Congress signed the Treaty of Geneva, which made the U. S. a member of the International Red Cross. Barton was appointed as the first president of the American Red Cross. She served in that position until May 1904. She died in Washington, D.C., on April 12, 1912.

ELIZABETH BLACKWELL (1821-1910) First Woman Medical Doctor in the U.S.

"When you want a thing deeply, earnestly and intensely, this feeling of desire reinforces your will and arises in you the determination to work for the desired object. When you have a distinct purpose in view, your work becomes of absorbing interest. You bend your best powers to it; you give it concentrated attention; you think of little else than the realization of this purpose; your will is stimulated into unusual activity, and as a consequence you do your work with an increasing sense of power."

Grenville Kleister

Elizabeth Blackwell's desire to become a medical doctor did not develop slowly. It occurred as a significant emotional event in her early twenties while visiting a friend who was dying of cancer. Her friend said to her, "You are fond of study, Elizabeth. You have health, leisure, and a cultivated intelligence. Why don't you devote these qualities to the service of suffering women? Why don't you study medicine? Had I been treated by a lady doctor, my worst sufferings would have been spared me."

Elizabeth considered the study of medicine. She knew that, although she was happy with her social life revolving around her parents, sisters, brothers, and friends in Cincinnati, it was not a fulfilling life for her. She did not feel challenged. She entered her personal reflections on pursuing the study of medicine in her diary: "The idea of winning a doctor's degree gradually assumed the aspect of a great moral struggle, and the moral fight possessed an immense attraction for me. This work has taken deep root in my soul and become an all-absorbing duty. I must accomplish my end. I consider it the noblest and most useful path that I can tread."

Before undertaking medical studies, Elizabeth had to earn money to finance her education. Her father, Samuel Blackwell, had passed away at the age of forty-eight, leaving the family in debt. Her mother, Hannah Lane Blackwell, Elizabeth, and her brothers and sisters had worked since Samuel's death to pay off family debts.

Blackwell taught school in Asheville, North Carolina, and then in Charleston, South Carolina, to earn money for medical school expenses. She sent out applications to medical schools while teaching in Charleston. She wanted to attend medical school in Philadelphia, which she considered the medical center of the United States because of its four highly regarded medical schools.

Blackwell sent her first inquiry to Dr. Joseph Warrington in Philadelphia. His response was discouraging; he viewed men as doctors and women as nurses and recommended that she pursue a nursing career. However, he added that, "if the project be of divine origin and appointment, it will sooner or later surely be accomplished." She applied to twenty-nine medical schools for admission and received twenty-eight rejections.

In late October 1847, Blackwell received an acceptance from the medical school of Geneva College, Geneva, New York. Dr. Benjamin Hale, President of Geneva College, was an open-minded individual who had recruited an extremely capable dean for the medical school, Dr. Charles Lee. The medical school later became part of Syracuse University and Geneva College was renamed Hobart College.

The circumstances surrounding Blackwell's acceptance were unusual. Dr. Warrington wrote a letter to Dr. Lee on her behalf. The Geneva faculty was unanimously against the admission of a woman to their medical school. However, they did not want to be responsible for rejecting the highly regarded Philadelphia doctor's request. The faculty turned the decision over to the medical students; they were confident that the students would vote against her admission.

Dr. Lee read Dr. Warrington's letter to the class and informed them that the faculty would let the students determine the issue. He told them that one negative vote would prevent Blackwell's admission. The students were enthusiastic about her admittance, and the single dissenting student was browbeaten into submission. She received a document composed by the students and signed by the chairman of the class:

1. Resolved—That one of the radical principles of a Republican Government is the universal education of both sexes; that to every branch of scientific education the door should be open equally to all; that the application of Elizabeth Blackwell to become a member of our class meets our entire approbation; and in extending our unanimous invitation we pledge ourselves that no conduct of ours shall cause her to regret her attendance at this institution.

2. Resolved—That a copy of these proceedings be signed by the chairman and transmitted to Elizabeth Blackwell.

T. J. Stratton, Chairman

Blackwell was overjoyed to receive the acceptance. She arrived in Geneva on November 6, having missed the first five weeks of the session. She was not sure what to expect from her fellow medical students; however, she had grown up with brothers and was not an overly sensitive young woman. She was well-mannered and dressed conservatively in Quaker style. The Geneva community was not ready for a female medical student, and, initially, she had difficulty finding a place to live. She moved into a drafty attic room in a boarding house and fed wood into a wood-burning stove to keep warm.

Eventually, Blackwell became aware that she was being subjected to a form of ostracism. The other boarders were unfriendly at mealtime, the women she passed on the street held their skirts to one side and did not speak, and one doctor's wife snubbed her openly. Her feelings were hurt by this treatment. She reacted by staying in her room and studying. Blackwell's Professor of Anatomy was Dr. James Webster, who was friendly and sincerely glad to have her in his class. He predicted: "You'll go through the course and get your diploma—with great éclat too. We'll give you the opportunities. You'll make a stir, I can tell you."

However, within a short time, he prevented Blackwell from attending a dissection. He wrote a note to her explaining that he was about to lecture on the reproductive organs and that he could not cover the material satisfactorily in the presence of a lady. He offered her the opportunity for dissection and study of this portion of the course in private. She knew that Dr. Webster had a reputation for being coarse in covering this material. He sprinkled his lecture with humorous anecdotes. The students liked this approach to the subject matter and responded by becoming somewhat rowdy.

Blackwell replied to Dr. Webster reminding him that she was a student with a serious purpose, and that she was aware of his awkward position, particularly "when viewed from the low standpoint of impure and unchaste sentiments." She asked why a student of science would have his mind diverted from such an absorbing subject by the presence of a student in feminine attire. She offered to remove her bonnet and sit in the back row of benches, but if the class wished she would not attend the class.

Dr. Webster acquiesced, and Blackwell attended the dissection, which was "just about as much as I could bear." She noted in her diary: "My delicacy was certainly shocked, and yet the exhibition was in some sense ludicrous. I had to pinch my hand until the blood nearly came, and call on Christ to help me from smiling, for that would have ruined everything; but I sat in grave indifference, though the effort made my heart palpitate most painfully." Dr. Webster conducted the class without the usual anecdotes.

Blackwell was a self-disciplined student who maintained a friendly but impersonal relationship with her classmates. She considered how to spend her summer adding to her medical knowledge. One of the few places open to her was Blockley Almshouse in Philadelphia, which cared for 2,000 unfortunates, most of whom were from the slums.

Again, Blackwell had to pay for being a pioneer. The resident doctors snubbed her and left a ward when she entered it. They neglected to enter the diagnosis and the notation of the medication used in treatment on the patients' charts. She had to make many of her own diagnoses. Her major accomplishment that summer was the preparation of a thesis on typhus for which she received compliments from senior staff physicians.

Blackwell worked hard during her second year of medical school. Although she had always received good grades, she approached her final exams with trepidation. When the results were compiled, Elizabeth had the best academic record in the class. However, the administration of Geneva College vacillated on establishing the precedent of awarding the first medical degree to a woman in the United States.

Dr. Webster defended her, saying, "She paid her tuition didn't she? She passed every course, each and every one with honors! And let me tell you, gentlemen, if you hold back, I'll take up a campaign in every medical journal." Blackwell received her medical degree on January 23, 1849. Her brother, Henry, traveled to Geneva to share the experience with her. She was invited to participate in the academic procession, which she declined "because it wouldn't be ladylike."

Blackwell was the last student called to receive a diploma from Dr. Hale. In presenting her diploma, Dr. Hale used the word *Domina* in place of *Domine*. Elizabeth replied, "Sir, I thank you. By the help of the Most High, it shall be the effort of my life to shed honor on your diploma."

Blackwell's brother, Henry, documented his recollections of the ceremony:

> He [Dr. Lee, who gave the valedictory address] pronounced her the leader of the class; stated that she had passed through a thorough course in every department, slighting none; that she had profited to the utmost by all the advantages of the institution, and by her ladylike and dignified deportment had proved that the strongest intellect and nerve, and the most untiring perseverance were compatible with the softest attributes of feminine delicacy and

grace, to all which the students manifested, by decided attempts at applause, their entire concurrence.

As Blackwell left the ceremony, the women of Geneva displayed their smiles and friendly faces to her. She was pleased to see this change in attitude; however, she recorded her true feelings in her diary: "For the next few hours, before I left by train, my room was thronged by visitors. I was glad of the sudden conversion thus shown, but my past experience had given me a useful and permanent lesson at the outset of life as to the very shallow nature of popularity."

Blackwell returned to Philadelphia with the hope of being accepted by the medical community there. She attended lectures at the University of Pennsylvania, but it was obvious that she was not going to be given the opportunity to gain the practical medical experience she needed. She went to Paris for further medical training, arriving on May 21, 1849 after a brief stay in England. Blackwell had forwarded a letter of introduction from a doctor in Boston to Dr. Pierre Louis, a highly regarded physician practicing in Paris. Her interview with Dr. Louis was not successful. He advised her to apply to La Maternité, a center for obstetrics where 3,000 babies were born annually. She realized that Dr. Louis viewed her as a midwife.

Blackwell's letter of introduction to Dr. Roux was more successful. She attended some of his lectures, and he took her on a tour of the wards of Hôtel Dieu. However, Dr. Henri Davanne, Director-general of the Paris hospitals, withdrew her permission to accompany physicians on their rounds at these hospitals, which was allowed for scores of male medical students. Dr. Paul DuBois and Dr. Armand Trousseau denied her permission to attend lectures at L'Ecole de Médecine. Dr. Trousseau suggested that she disguise herself as a man. She had heard this recommendation before, and she was no more receptive of the idea now than she had been previously. However, lectures at the College de France and the Jardin des Plantes were open to her.

In late June, Blackwell was accepted into La Maternité, due mainly to the efforts of the U.S. Ambassador to Turkey, who happened to be visiting in Paris. Even with this diplomatic assistance, she was accepted as an aide, not as a doctor. She lived in a dormitory with sixteen young, exuberant French girls from the provinces who were there to be trained as aides. She made the best of her circumstances and used every opportunity to add to her medical knowledge.

In October 1850, Blackwell returned to London and was pleased to hear that the medical council at St. Bartholomew's Hospital had approved her application for further study. Dr. James Paget, the distinguished surgeon, made a point of making her welcome. She had access to every department of the hospital except the department of female diseases, which was the decision of the Professor of Midwifery; he had nothing against her personally but felt that he could not approve of "a lady's studying medicine."

Upon completion of additional training abroad, Blackwell returned to New York and attempted to establish herself with the medical community. She was not accepted as she had been in London. Her application to work as an assistant physician in the department for women and children at a city dispensary was rejected. She requested permission to visit the women's ward of one of the city hospitals, and her request was ignored. She was advised to open her own dispensary.

Finally, Blackwell used half of her savings to furnish a set of rooms where she had to pay an inflated rent. The New York *Tribune* carried the announcement that Dr. Elizabeth Blackwell had opened an office and was accepting patients. Elizabeth's landlady contributed to her difficulty in establishing her practice. She indicated her disapproval of Elizabeth's profession by refusing to deliver messages to her.

Blackwell expressed her thoughts in a letter to her younger sister, Emily, who planned to follow in her sister's footsteps: "A blank wall of social and professional antagonism faces the woman physician that forms a situation of singular and painful loneliness, leaving her without support, respect, or professional counsel."

Blackwell planned, wrote, and delivered a series of six lectures. In the lectures, she advocated more varied and extended education for women, increased physical activity for women including participation in sports, and health and hygiene courses for young women. She wrote a book incorporating many of the thoughts in her lectures. In late 1852, it was published as *The Laws of Life with Special Reference to the Physical Education of Girls.*

Although Blackwell's views about hygiene were gaining acceptance, she was jeered while walking around the city. She received not only scorn but also threatening letters. She was viewed as a person who lectured about subjects that should not be discussed in public. She was bothered most by women who would not consider having a woman doctor.

Blackwell wanted to do more than run a dispensary. She wanted to establish a hospital to care for the sick who were unable to pay for treatment, to educate women physicians, and to train nurses. She was forced to close her dispensary because the $5,000 she needed to continue was not available in 1855, a recession year. Finally, she bought a house in which to establish her hospital. Her sister, Emily, who had received her medical degree at Western Reserve University in Ohio, had received further medical training in Europe and was now a trained surgeon. Emily was eager to join the staff of the fledgling hospital.

Dr. Henry Ward Beecher, brother of Harriet Beecher Stowe, author of *Uncle Tom's Cabin*, spoke at the official opening of the New York Infirmary for Women and Children on May 12, 1857:

> Woman should be entirely a better physician than man. Her intuition, perception, and good mother wit should make her so. Indeed, she is particularly fitted for the study of medicine.... Besides, woman has a right to do whatever she can do well, and I welcome anything that tends to enlarge the sphere of her development. I am sure this Infirmary will grow and prosper. I expect to see it as one of the giant institutions of the land.

Charles A. Dana, Cyrus W. Field, and Horace Greeley were trustees of the Infirmary.

In 1858, Blackwell traveled to England, where she became the first woman in the British Medical Register. She never wavered from her goal of establishing a medical college for women; nevertheless, she had to postpone her efforts due to the demands of the Civil War from 1861 to 1864. She assisted the war effort by selecting candidates for nursing training, whom she trained at one of the New York hospitals or her Infirmary, equipped them, and forwarded them to Dorothea Dix, Superintendent of Nurses, in Washington, D.C. In 1866, Blackwell established the first visiting nurse program in New York City.

In November 1868, Blackwell opened her medical college. For thirty-one years, the college filled a need in providing medical education for women. In 1899, it was incorporated into the Cornell Medical Center. A separate medical college for women was no longer required; qualified women could obtain admittance to other medical colleges. The infirmary continued to exist as a separate entity.

Blackwell returned to England in 1869, where she assisted with women's efforts in Britain to enter the medical profession. In 1870, she helped to found the British National Health Society. In 1876, she accepted a teaching position in gynecology at the London School for Women. Her book, *The Moral Education of the Young*, was published that year.

Blackwell's niece, Anna, said, "I stood in awe of her although she was sweet and serene. One felt she had conquered so much.... Like her father, she had a sense of fun, but she had a masterful persistence when she felt she was right." Dr. Elizabeth Cushier, a peer of Elizabeth and Emily, observed:

> We may forget the early struggles of the doctors Elizabeth and Emily Blackwell, but what we should never forget is that the dignity, the culture, and the high moral standards which formed their character, finally prevailed in overcoming the

existing prejudice, both within and outside the profession. By their standards, the status of women in
medicine was determined.

The infirmary founded by Elizabeth Blackwell is now New
York Downtown Hospital. In 1899, Hobart and William Smith
Colleges, successors to Geneva College, named its first residence
hall for women Blackwell House. In 1926, the London School of
Medicine paid tribute to Geneva College as having the "highest
ideals of American justice and liberty in inaugurating a new era in
the story of medical science by conferring on a woman the degree
of M.D." Elizabeth Blackwell overcame all of the obstacles
encountered by a pioneer. She was determined and courageous.

EMMELINE AND CHRISTABEL PANKHURST
(1858-1928, 1880-1958) Women's Rights Leaders in England

"There was something quite ruthless about Mrs. Pankhurst and Christabel where human relationships were concerned . . . Men and women of destiny are like that."

Emmeline Pethick-Lawrence

Emmeline Pankhurst and her daughters played a major role in the Women's Suffrage Movement in England, which was much more militant than the movement in the United States. Women realized that the only way to gain their rights, particularly the right to vote, was to organize protest marches and to destroy public property to get the attention of the government. Unlike women in the United States, when English women finally obtained the right to vote, it was granted in stages. Emmeline, who was born in 1858, was the attractive, delicate eldest daughter of Robert Goulden, a wealthy cotton printer from Manchester. After returning from finishing school in Paris in 1878, Emmeline met Richard Pankhurst, a radical advocate who had been called to the Bar in 1867 after receiving the highest law degrees at London University.

In 1865, when Emmeline was only seven years old, Pankhurst had helped to found the Woman's Suffrage Society in Manchester. In 1870, he had drafted the Married Women's Property Bill that gave women the right to own property and to keep the wages they earned. Also that year, he drafted the first of many parliamentary bills to give women the right to vote.

Emmeline and Richard fell in love at first sight. She was captivated by his eloquence, his idealism, and his "beautiful white hands." They had a happy marriage, partly because they saw each other as kindred spirits ("Every struggling cause shall be ours").

Four children were born during the first six years of their marriage: Christabel in 1880, Sylvia in 1882, Adela in 1885, and a son who died in childhood. Pankhurst thought of his four children as the four pillars of his home. He repeatedly told them that if they didn't grow up to help other people, they would not have been worth the upbringing. He continually counseled them that drudgery and drill are important elements of life, but that "life is nothing without enthusiasms." The Pankhursts were politically active in Manchester. They were active Socialists as well as feminists. Women's rights was Pankhurst's highest priority, and he was a strong influence on his wife and daughters. As one who opposed exploitation of all kinds, he couldn't tolerate half of the population being held back economically and politically. Financial problems plagued the family. Years of overwork caught up with Pankhurst; he developed gastric ulcers.

In 1890, the usually calm Pankhurst erupted after a meeting of the Women's Franchise League in their home. He burst out, "Why don't you force us to give you the vote? Why don't you scratch our eyes out?" Christabel and Sylvia were startled by his outburst; Emmeline was astonished at the vehemence of his feelings.

In 1895, Emmeline was elected to the Chorlton Board of Guardians. When she was told that the Guardians couldn't provide relief to the "able bodied poor," she organized food kitchens. She was horrified by conditions in the workhouses and incensed by the treatment of young women with illegitimate babies. Years later, she wrote that although she had been a suffragist before, she began to view the women's vote not only as a right, but as a vital necessity.

In 1898, Richard Pankhurst died suddenly of a perforated ulcer, leaving no money to the family. Pankhurst had frequently asked his children what they wanted to be when they grew up. He had always advised them to work at something that they liked to do and could do well. However, at the time of his death, none of the children was educated or trained to help their mother support the family. Eighteen-year-old Christabel had considered both ballet dancing and dressmaking, but she wasn't encouraged to do either.

Emmeline accepted a position as Registrar of Births and Deaths with the Chorlton Board of Guardians. Christabel enrolled in courses at the University of Manchester, where she participated in discussions. Her perceptive responses brought her to the attention of Eva Gore-Booth and Esther Roper of the Suffrage Movement.

After the death of Lydia Decker, their dynamic leader, the suffragists in England were divided about the amount of political involvement that they should have. Lydia's successor was Millicent Fawcett, a capable leader but one without Lydia's drive. Eva and Esther, who were looking for dynamic women to work in the Movement, asked Christabel to join their cause.

Emmeline's interest in the Suffrage Movement was elevated by her daughter's participation; she worked actively for the Women's Rights Movement, thereby establishing an extraordinary mother-daughter partnership.

Christabel discovered that she was a natural leader and speaker. Her intelligence, pleasant appearance, and forceful personality impressed her audiences. Christabel had an internal need to dominate her environment. The Suffrage Movement provided her with a forum to display her strengths.

In 1903, Emmeline invited Labour Party women to a meeting at her home and founded the Women's Social and Political Union (WSPU). Their motto was "Deeds, not Words"; their slogan was "Votes for Women." For the next eleven years, the WSPU disseminated the views of this remarkable mother-daughter partnership.

Many English women were upset with the government. They realized that relying on private Members' bills wasn't the path to success; the government must legislate. An attempt was made to pass a bill to help the unemployed in an economy with increasing unemployment. Prime Minister Balfour's government attempted to postpone the bill. Several thousand destitute workers marched from the East End to Westminster in protest. In Manchester, mobs of enraged unemployed men marched in the streets, and four men were arrested. ten days later, Arthur Balfour backed down,and the bill became law.

This success was not lost on the women of the WSPU. They realized that the threat of violence had caused the government to act. If a threat of violence was required to get bills passed into law, then they would become increasingly militant. The Pankhursts spearheaded a nationwide militant movement operating out of Manchester and led by Christabel.

Esther Roper, who was impressed with Christabel's skill in arguing issues, suggested to Emmeline that her oldest daughter should study law. Christabel enrolled at Manchester University's law school, while continuing to participate in suffrage work.

Christabel's coworker, Annie Kenny, wondered where and how she studied because she worked for the Movement every day and almost every night. However, as her final examination approached, Christabel withdrew from all other activities to concentrate on preparing for it. In June 1906, she graduated with honors and used her new skills to support the women's cause. Christabel focused on one overriding issue—obtaining the vote for women. All other causes, including social reform issues, would have to wait.

Christabel's first unladylike step occurred in 1904 at a Liberal Party meeting at the Free Trade Hall in Manchester during which Winston Churchill launched the campaign for the general election. When a resolution supporting free trade was agreed upon and the speeches were over, Christabel rose from her chair on the platform and asked the chairman if she could propose an amendment on women's suffrage. The chairman denied her request amid cries from the audience, and Christabel backed down.

Later, she recalled, "This was the first militant step—the hardest for me because it was the first. To move from my place on the platform to the speaker's table in the teeth of the astonishment and opposition of the will of that immense throng, those civic and county leaders and those Members of Parliament, was the most difficult thing I have ever done." Nevertheless, it was "a protest of which little was heard and nothing remembered—because it did not result in imprisonment!" She formed the opinion that she must go to prison to arouse public opinion; she must become a martyr.

In 1905, Christabel and Annie Kenney attended a Liberal Party rally in Manchester. Christabel had told her mother, "We shall sleep in prison tonight." They carried a banner that asked "Will you give votes for women?" Both Annie and Christabel asked the question on their banner. The Chief Constable of Manchester told them that their question would be answered later. It was ignored, so they asked it again. The crowd responded, "Throw them out!" Stewards bruised and scratched them while attempting to remove them from the hall.

Christabel realized that they hadn't done enough to be taken to prison. She knew that she was going to have to do more to be arrested; however, she wasn't sure how to do that with her arms being held behind her back. Finally, she was arrested and charged with "spitting at a policeman."

Her account of the incident was, "It was not a real spit, but only, shall we call it, a 'pout,' a perfectly dry purse of the mouth. I could not really have done it, even to get the vote, I think." Christabel was kept in jail for seven days; Annie was jailed for three days. Christabel received the publicity that she sought.

Sylvia Pankhurst and Annie interrupted a speech in Sheffield by Henry Asquith, Chancellor of the Exchequer, and were jostled by the stewards. Men in the crowd hit them with fists and umbrellas as the women were roughly forced from the hall. The Pankhursts decided to spread their activities to London. Unfortunately, they didn't have the finances to do it. They sent Annie Kenney to London with £2 in her pocketbook to spread their version of militant suffrage activity. Emmeline Pankhurst instructed her to "go and rouse London."

The necessary financing did come to them. Frederick and Emmeline ("the other Emmeline") Pethick-Lawrence were visiting South Africa when they heard of the suffragist activities in England. They hurried home to see what they could do to help. The Pethick-Lawrences were philanthropists who had contributed to university settlements and women's hospitals and had founded boys' clubs. They expanded the scope of their monthly newspaper, the *Labour Record*, from supporting the Labour Party cause to supporting the Suffrage Movement.

Initially, Emmeline Pethick-Lawrence hesitated before backing the Pankhursts. In her autobiography, she observed, "I had no fancy to be drawn into a small group of brave and reckless and quite helpless people who were prepared to dash themselves against the oldest tradition of human civilization as well as one of the strongest governments of modern times." She was moved by Annie Kenney's willingness to "rouse London" with £2 in her pocketbook. "I was amused by Annie's ignorance of what the talk of rousing London would involve and yet thrilled by her courage."

The "other Emmeline" attended a suffrage meeting at Sylvia Pankhurst's lodgings and was impressed with the audacity of the six women who were there. Pethick-Lawrence said, "I found there was no office, no organization, no money—no postage stamps even.... It was not without dismay that it was borne on me that somebody had to come to the help of this brave little group, and that the finger of fate pointed to me." Emmeline Pethick-Lawrence helped to establish the Central Committee of the WSPU and became its honorary treasurer.

Not only was Emmeline Pethick-Lawrence an effective treasurer; she was also a source of many good ideas. Money began to flow into the Movement, including generous contributions from Frederick Pethick-Lawrence. The Pethick-Lawrences allowed the Pankhursts to use their house at Clements Inn as their base of operations, retaining only the upstairs apartment for their own use in addition to one room as an office for the *Labour Record*. They treated Christabel as a favored daughter.

The *Daily Mail* called the militant suffragists "suffragettes," a name that Christabel liked. In her opinion, the suffragists merely desired the vote, but, if you pronounce the hard "g," the suffragettes "mean to get it." Membership in the WSPU grew rapidly. Middle class women joined because they were looking for "wider and more important activities and interests." Women of the upper class were drawn to the WSPU for other reasons: "Daughters of rich families were often without personal means, or permitted a meager dress allowance, and when their parents died, they were often reduced to genteel penury, or unwelcome dependence on relatives.... It offered an outlet from an empty, purposeless existence to an active, exciting part in ... the most important work in the world."

The command of the Movement became a triumvirate: Christabel and the two Emmelines. There was no question as to who was in charge; it was Christabel. Emmeline Pankhurst willingly followed the direction of her oldest daughter.

In early 1906, thirty women carrying banners marched in front of the residence of the Chancellor of the Exchequer, Henry Asquith. The marchers were punched and kicked by police, who attempted to break up the march. Annie Kenney and two other suffragettes were sent to jail for six weeks, and Emmeline Pankhurst was handled roughly for asking a question at one of Asquith's meetings. In October 1906, ten women were arrested for making speeches in the lobby of Parliament.

Prisons had three divisions or levels of treatment. In the Third Division, the lowest division, the women were considered common criminals. They ate prison food, were subjected to coarse treatment, and wore prison clothing. Treatment in the Second Division was marginally better. Prisoners in the First Division enjoyed many privileges, including the right to have friends visit, to wear their own clothing, and to have food, writing materials, and other amenities from the outside world.

In 1907, the triumvirate called a Women's Parliament near Westminster to coincide with the opening of Parliament. When they heard that there had been no mention of women's suffrage in the King's Speech, 400 women stormed Parliament. Sylvia described the activities of the constables:

> Mounted men scattered the marchers; foot police seized them by the back of the neck and rushed them along at arm's length, thumping them in the back, and bumping them with their knees in approved police fashion. Women, by the hundred, returned again and again with painful persistence, enduring this treatment by the hour. Those who took refuge in doorways were dragged down by the steps and hurled in front of the horses, then pounced on by the constables and beaten again.

Fifty women were arrested, including Christabel. Sentences ranged from one to three weeks. This time, the women were placed in the First Division.

In 1908 at the by-election in mid-Devon, Emmeline Pankhurst and a fellow suffragist were attacked by a gang of young Liberal toughs, who were unhappy that their candidate had lost to the Tory candidate. Mrs. Pankhurst was knocked unconscious into the mud and injured her ankle. The young toughs were about to stuff her into a barrel and roll her down main street, when she was rescued by mounted police. The effects of the ankle injury persisted for months and motivated her to work harder to obtain the vote.

Christabel decided that the next step was for her mother to go to jail. From a small cart, the injured Emmeline led a delegation of thirteen women who marched on Parliament. The thirteen women were sent to prison for six months in the Second Division. In her first visit to prison, Emmeline tolerated the stripping, the body search, the bath in filthy water, and the patched and stained prison clothing made of coarse material.

She knew that the cold cells and the plank bed would be uncomfortable, but she was unprepared for the sobbing and foul language of the other prisoners. In particular, she was affected by the claustrophobic living conditions of many women in a small cell. Within two days, dyspepsia, migraine headaches, and neuralgia caused her to be moved to the prison hospital.

Another march on Parliament was planned. They weren't sure which verb to use. They considered "besiege," "invade," "raid," and "storm," and finally settled on "rush," which was enough of an action word to provoke the government. They circulated leaflets with the message, "Men and Women—Help the Suffragettes to Rush the House of Commons," and Christabel and Emmeline spoke in Trafalgar Square. Their call to action was heard by Lloyd George, Chancellor of the Exchequer, and they were charged with "inciting the public to a certain wrongful and illegal act—to rush the House of Commons."

Christabel conducted her own defense at her trial at Bow Street. The magistrate rejected her request for a trial by jury; nevertheless, she called Lloyd George and Herbert Gladstone, the Home Secretary, as witnesses. The public was captivated by a young woman lawyer cross-examining Cabinet Ministers. The

Suffrage Movement received much publicity, but, after two days, Emmeline was sentenced to three months in the Second Division and Christabel to ten weeks.

During the trial, writer Max Beerbohm was impressed with Christabel. He wrote in the *Saturday Review*: "She has all the qualities which an actress needs and of which so few actresses have any.... Her whole being is alive with her every meaning, and if you can imagine a very graceful rhythmic dance done by a dancer who uses not her feet, you will have some idea of Miss Pankhurst's method." Furthermore, he noted "the contrast between the buoyancy of the girl and the depression of the statesman [Lloyd George]."

During a rally at Albert Hall where Lloyd George spoke, the suffragettes were abused again. They were bruised, and their clothing was disarranged. Some had their corsets ripped off and their false teeth knocked out. One woman had been whipped with a dog whip, and another had a wrist burned by a man using it to put out his cigar while other men struck her in the chest. The Manchester *Guardian* reported that the women had been treated "with a brutality that was almost nauseating."

The more activist members of the Movement began to become impatient with the government's delays. They threw stones wrapped in WSPU literature through the windows of government buildings. When they were arrested, they went on hunger strikes. Women who were prevented from attending public meetings climbed onto the roof of the hall and used axes to chop off slates. One woman was imprisoned for throwing an iron bar through the window of an empty railroad car on the train carrying the Prime Minister to London.

Women were given sentences ranging from two weeks to four months. Many of them went on hunger strikes. The Home Secretary ordered that they be forcibly fed using rubber tubes through their mouth or nose. In one case, the feeding tube was accidentally passed into the trachea instead of the esophagus, and the woman developed pneumonia from broth forced into her lung.

Sylvia Pankhurst described being forcibly fed in graphic terms. She experienced shivering and heart palpitations when told that she was going to be forcibly fed. Six big, strong wardresses pushed her down on her back in bed and held her by her ankles, knees, hips, elbows, and shoulders.

A doctor entered her room and attempted unsuccessfully to open her mouth. He then tried to push a steel gag through a gap between her teeth, making her gums bleed. Next two doctors thrust a pointed steel instrument between her jaws, which were forced open by the turn of a screw, and pushed a tube down her throat. While Sylvia panted and heaved, she tried to move her head away. She was almost unconscious when they poured the broth into her throat. As soon as the tube was withdrawn, she vomited. She said, "They left me on the bed exhausted, gasping for breath, and sobbing convulsively." The women were subjected to this treatment twice a day.

Some women died for their beliefs in the women's cause. In December 1910, Celia Haig, a sturdy, healthy woman, died of a painful illness from injuries incurred when she was assaulted at a public gathering. Mary Clarke, Emmeline Pankhurst's sister, died of a stroke after being released from prison "too frail to weather this rude tide of militant struggle." Henria Williams, who had a weak heart, died in January 1911 from injuries suffered during a rally.

Early in 1912, Emmeline Pankhurst broke several windows at the Prime Minister's residence at 10 Downing Street. She went to jail for two months with 218 other women. In March 1912, the police raided WSPU headquarters and arrested Emmeline and Frederick Pethick-Lawrence. Christabel had recently moved into an apartment and wasn't at Clements Inn when the police arrived. It was obvious to Christabel that the "ringleaders" were being rounded up. She fled to France to ensure that the Movement's leaders weren't all in jail. Annie Kenney became her link with Clements Inn.

Frederick and the two Emmelines were sent to prison for seven months in the Second Division. Emmeline Pankhurst refused to be treated as she had been on her first trip to prison. Sylvia described the scene: "Mrs. Pankhurst, ill from fasting and suspense, grasped the earthen toilet ewer and threatened to fling it at the doctors and wardresses, who appeared with the feeding tube. They withdrew and the order for her release was issued the next day." Emmeline Pethick-Lawrence was forcibly fed once, and her husband for five days; they, too, were released early.

The militant wing of the Movement set fire to buildings, including churches, historic places, and empty buildings. They tried to set fire to Nuneham House, the home of Lewis Harcourt, an anti-suffragist Minister. Mary Leigh and Gladys Evans attempted to burn down the Royal Theatre in Dublin, where Herbert Asquith was scheduled to speak.

Christabel's mother convinced her that increased militancy was the direction in which they should move. This caused a rift with the Pethick-Lawrences, who preferred a more moderate approach. When they returned from a trip to Canada, the couple who had contributed so much to the campaign found that they had been forced out of the leadership.

Frederick commented on their falling out in unselfish terms: "Thus ended our personal association with two of the most remarkable women I have ever known.... They cannot be judged by ordinary standards of conduct; and those who run up against them must not complain of the treatment they receive." Emmeline Pethick-Lawrence did not accept the split with the Pankhursts as easily as her husband did. She was offended by being dumped by them after contributing so much time and money to their mutual cause.

However, Frederick and Emmeline Pethick-Lawrence recognized Christabel's intelligence and political acumen as well as her appeal to young men and women. They also appreciated Mrs. Pankhurst's ability to move an audience with her appeals to their emotions by modulating her voice.

The level of destruction caused by the suffragettes stepped up as they became increasingly frustrated with the delay in obtaining the vote. Their acts included:

- widespread burning with acid of the message "votes for women" on golf greens
- cutting telephone wires

- burning boathouses and sports pavilions, including the grandstand at Ayr Racecourse
- slashing thirteen paintings at the Manchester Art Gallery and the Rokeby *Venus* at the National Gallery
- destroying with a bomb a home being built for Lloyd George
- smashing the glass orchid house at Kew Gardens
- breaking a jewel case in the Tower of London
- burning three Scottish castles and the Carnegie Library in Birmingham
- flooding the organ in Albert Hall
- exploding a bomb in Westminster Abbey

Emmeline Pankhurst was charged with "counseling and procuring" the bombing of the house being constructed for Lloyd George at Walton-on-the-Hill. That bombing was done by Emily Wilding Davison, one of the most impulsive suffragettes. To protest not being granted the vote, Emily waited at the turn at Tattenham Corner and committed suicide by later throwing herself under the King's horse at the Derby.

The militancy of the Movement in England ceased with the outbreak of World War I. Christabel moved back to England, confident that the government would have more on its mind than pursuing her. She announced, "This was national militancy. As suffragettes we could not be pacifists at any price. We offered our service to the country and called upon all our members to do likewise." Christabel supported Prime Minister Asquith in the war effort as fervently as she had opposed him prior to the war.

In August 1916, Asquith surprised the House of Commons by declaring that if the voting franchise were expanded, women had an "unanswerable" case for obtaining the vote. He said that "during this war, the women of this country have rendered as effective a service in the prosecution of the war as any other class of the community."

In February 1917, a committee recommended that the vote be granted to all men over twenty-one and women over thirty who were university graduates or local government electors (owners or tenant householders), or the wives of both. The bill was extended to the wives of all voters and became law in January 1918. Eight and a half million women were enfranchised. Ten years later, the remaining political limitations on women were removed.

Emmeline Pankhurst died in June 1928, a month before her seventieth birthday. Christabel wrote, "The House of Lords passed the final measure of Votes for Women in the hour her body, which had suffered so much for that cause, was laid in the grave. She, who had come to them in their need, had stayed with the women as long as they might still need her, and then she went away."

Christabel became a Second Adventist and in 1936 was made a Dame Commander of the British Empire for "public and social services." She moved to the United States and died in Santa Monica, California in 1958.

The courageous Pankhursts were a family of achievers. Perhaps the single characteristic that most led to their many accomplishments was best summarized by Frederick and Emmeline Pethick-Lawrence: "Their absolute refusal to be deflected by criticism or appeal one hair's breadth from the course they had determined to pursue."

ALICE PAUL (1885-1977) American Social Reformer

"She [Alice Paul] has in the first place a devotion to the cause which is absolutely self-sacrificing. She has an indomitable will. She recognizes no obstacles. She has a clear, penetrating, analytic mind which cleaves straight to the heart of things. In examining a situation, she always bares the main fact; she sees all the forces which make for change in that situation. She is a genius for organization, both in the mass and in the detail. She understands perfectly, in achieving the big object, the cumulative effect of multitudes of small actions and small services. She makes use of all material, whether human or otherwise, that comes along . . . Her inventiveness and resourcefulness are endless."

Maud Younger, suffragist

Alice Paul organized the picketing and the suffrage parades in Washington, D.C. She didn't mind getting her hands dirty and being thrown in jail to aid the cause of obtaining the right to vote for women. In her later years, she was an active sponsor of the Equal Rights Amendment.

Alice Paul was born in Moorestown, New Jersey, in 1885 to upper-middle-class Quaker parents. Her father was a successful farmer and banker. She attended the Friends' elementary and high school in Moorestown and then enrolled in Swarthmore College, which her grandparents had helped to found. She had read English literature and history widely, so she majored in biology, a subject about which she knew little.

In her senior year at Swarthmore, Paul's interest shifted to economics and political science. After graduating, she was awarded a one-year graduate scholarship at the School of Philanthropy in New York, which later became part of Columbia University. Her fellowship involved work in the College Settlement, which was her first exposure to a heterogeneous group of people. In fact, 1905-06 was a peak of immigration to the United States, and the lower East Side of Manhattan was truly a melting pot.

Paul received a degree in social work and completed a number of assignments in the field, which was one of the few majors other than nursing and teaching open to women at the time. The following year, she received a Master's degree at the University of Pennsylvania with a major in sociology and a double minor in economics and political science.

In 1907, Paul went to England to study on a fellowship at the Quakers' Woodbrooke Institute. She enrolled in Woodbrooke's combined program at the University of Birmingham, which consisted of courses in economics and training in social work. Her fellowship included work at the Summer Lane Settlement. Her lifelong career decision was made, or was thrust upon her, while she was a student at the University of Birmingham.

Paul attended a public meeting sponsored by the University. She described the experience:

> So I went to this public meeting—after school hours, you see. It was Christabel Pankhurst. I don't know that I had ever heard her name before.... She was [suffrage leader] Mrs. Pankhurst's daughter.... She was a very young girl and a young lawyer.... Quite an entrancing and delightful person, really very beautiful I thought. So she started to speak. And the students started to yell and shout, and I don't believe anybody heard one single word that Christabel said. So she kept on anyway for her whole speech. She was completely shouted down.
>
> So I just became from that moment very anxious to help in this movement.... I thought, "That's one group now that I want to throw in all the strength I can give to help.

When Paul finished the program at the Woodbrooke Institute, she enrolled at the London School of Economics. She joined the Women's Social and Political Union, did some administrative work for the Pankhursts, and marched in a large suffrage parade through London.

Paul learned how to speak in public, usually on street corners, and how to sell the idea of "votes for women." She also learned how to use the cry "votes for women" to disrupt the speeches of the British political leaders. She was sent to prison three times, where she engaged in a hunger strike and was forcibly fed. She soon became an assistant to Mrs. Pankhurst.

At the London School of Economics, Paul's own social thinking was evolving. She was influenced by Professor Westermark, a Dutch anthropologist, who wrote the classic book, *The History of Human Marriage*. Paul concluded that there were certain female traits that were evident in all cultures that distinguished women's personality characteristics and motivations from those of men.

In 1910, Paul declined a paid position with Mrs. Pankhurst and returned to the United States, where she worked with the Philadelphia suffrage organization. She enrolled in graduate school at the University of Pennsylvania and received a PhD degree in June 1912. Her interests were widening into the field of law, and her doctoral dissertation was "The Legal Position of Women in Pennsylvania."

Later that year, Paul worked with Jane Addams and became chair of the Congressional Committee of the National American Woman Suffrage Association (NAWSA). The NAWSA's emphasis had been to get suffrage referenda passed in all forty-eight states. Her role was to push for a women's suffrage amendment to the Constitution. These were difficult times for the Suffrage Movement; referenda had failed to pass in several states, which wasn't surprising since only men could vote.

Paul organized a large suffrage parade in the nation's capital; boisterous crowds caused considerable disorder along the parade route. The cavalry was called out to control the rowdy counter-demonstrators. Paul then mobilized women voters in the western states, who had already been granted the right to vote, to hold Woodrow Wilson and the Democrats—the party in power—responsible for their failure to obtain the elective franchise for women.

Paul established a new organization, the Congressional Union, to push for a women's suffrage amendment. The NAWSA would not allow it to be an auxiliary of their organization; so she split her organization off from the NAWSA. The Congressional Union evolved into the National Woman's Party. In 1917, she organized women picketers who carried bright purple, white, and gold anti-Wilson banners outside the grounds of the White House. When mobs attacked the suffragists, police arrested the women. In prison, she and the other courageous suffragists went on hunger strikes and were forcibly fed.

Paul was allowed no visitors in prison, not even her lawyer. Also, she was not permitted to receive mail. Prison psychiatrists interviewed her several times. They asked her questions about her feelings toward President Wilson, and, in particular, if she considered him her enemy. They told her that one signature on an admission form was all that was required to commit her to an insane asylum.

Visits from the head physician of the District of Columbia jail were particularly threatening to Paul. She admitted that "I believe I have never in my life before feared anything or any human being. But I confess I was afraid of Dr. Gannon, the jail physician. I dreaded the hour of his visit. He said, 'I will show you who rules this place. You think you do. But I will show you that you are wrong.'"

After her release from jail, Paul, with the help of a capable staff, directed the fund-raising, lobbying, and publicity efforts of her growing organization. She was good at fund-raising; Mrs. Alva Vanderbilt Belmont was a major contributor. President Wilson's government felt the increasing pressure of their activity. The work of the National Woman's Party was called "militant," but Paul considered it "nonviolent." She counseled her picketers to dress well and not to indulge in conduct unbecoming a lady, such as screaming. Their efforts were viewed by the courts as civil disobedience because their picketing was considered "obstructing traffic."

Paul focused her organization on women's right to vote. She believed in wider social reform, but, in order to concentrate her effort on obtaining the elective franchise for women, she did not work toward other reform objectives, such as child labor laws, equal pay for equal work for women, or welfare. Although she looked forward to the end of World War I, she was not distracted by the peace movement. From 1916 to 1920, the NAWSA, the organization from which Alice had broken off, also pushed forcefully for a women's suffrage amendment.

In August 1920, American women were granted the right to vote. Paul and her staff were exhausted. However, she continued to work to pay off the debts of the National Woman's Party. She also worked to get discriminatory laws replaced in several states. She earned three degrees in jurisprudence by attending classes early in the morning and in the evening.

Paul began to work toward an Equal Rights Amendment, which was submitted to Congress for the first time in 1923. She worked with women attorneys to document the laws affecting the family and women in all states to show the need for a federal Equal Rights Amendment. Not all reformers were in favor of an amendment, partly because of its potential impact on protective labor legislation. Some feared that hard-fought legislation for women such as maximum hours, minimum wage, restrictions on hours of work at night, and limitations on the weight workers could be required to lift might be lost or watered down.

In the 1920s, Paul and the National Woman's Party pushed to expand the concept of equal rights beyond the United States. In Paris, Mrs. Alva Vanderbilt Belmont corresponded with forty-five feminists in twenty-six countries to form an International Advisory Council of the National Woman's Party.

In 1926, the National Woman's Party joined the Open Door Council, an equal rights group based in England. Two years later the Party attended the Sixth Pan-American Conference in Havana, at which the Inter-American Commission of Women was established. Paul was appointed to head a committee to prepare a survey of all member nations' laws for nationality requirements. The comprehensive document was called "Alice Paul's Golden Book" by James Brown Scott, an authority on international law.

In 1928, the National Woman's Party participated in a meeting of the Open Door Council in Berlin at which a Charter of Economic Rights for Working Women was prepared. The Open Door Council opened an international office in Geneva to track the activities of the League of Nations and the International Labor Office. During the 1930s, the International Advisory Committee of the National Woman's Party worked for equal rights.

In 1938, Paul was a driving force in establishing the World Woman's Party, which was modeled on the National Woman's Party, to concentrate on equal rights for women in international rights and treaties. The headquarters, near the League of Nations and the International Red Cross in Geneva, became a refuge for women and their families fleeing the battlefields after World War II began in Europe in 1939. She shifted her efforts to the resettling of refugees.

After World War II, Paul continued to push for the passage of the Equal Rights Amendment in the U.S. She ensured that it was introduced in each session of Congress until 1972, when it passed from Congress to the states for ratification. Alice Paul died in 1977. That year ratification was three states short of passage.

Alice Paul's contributions to the Women's Rights Movement will always be remembered, particularly her work to keep the pressure on President Wilson and his administration to support women's suffrage. Like Susan B. Anthony, Alice Paul never married but devoted her entire career to the Women's Rights Movement and social reform.

CHAPTER 5

VICTORS / LEADERS

"Unbounded courage and compassion joined, tempering each other in the victor's mind, alternately proclaim good and great, and make the hero and the man complete."

Joseph Addison, *The Campaign*

ROBERT BRUCE (1274-1329) King Robert I of Scotland

"The greatest test of courage on earth is to endure defeat without losing heart."

R. G. Ingersoll, *The Declaration of Independence*

In 1305 and early 1306, Scotland was ruled by Edward I of England, a strong, cruel Plantagenet king. Scotland had been a conquered country, or at least partly under English control, since 1296. The Scottish patriot, William Wallace, tried to throw off the English yoke with a rousing victory at Stirling Bridge in September 1297, but his forces lost the battle of Falkirk to the English longbow the following July and were reduced to guerrilla actions. Wallace was a commoner with no aspirations to the crown of Scotland.

In 1306, the two Scottish lords with the greatest claim to the throne were John Comyn of Badenoch, "the Red Comyn," who was the nephew of the previous king, John Balliol, and Robert Bruce, whose grandfather had been King of Scotland. John Comyn had been in communication with Edward I of England. When Robert Bruce heard of these discussions, he suggested that Comyn meet with him in the Church of the Minorite Friars in Dumfries.

The heirs to the throne argued heatedly near the high altar, and Robert Bruce fatally stabbed the Red Comyn. Bruce's companions claimed that it was self-defense. Bruce was concerned about losing the support of the Church by this act but was pardoned by the patriotic Bishop of Glasgow, Bishop Wishart. On Palm Sunday, 1306, Bruce was crowned Robert I, King of Scotland, at Scone.

Scotland was a divided country, and many Scottish lords sided with the English. Bruce's early encounters with the English and their Scottish allies were a series of defeats. In June 1306, he was routed at the battle of Methven in his first battle as King of Scotland. During the battle, Bruce was taken prisoner briefly but was rescued by his brother-in-law, Christopher Seton. Bishop Wishart was captured and imprisoned. Six of the knights who had supported Bruce at his coronation were captured, and sixteen nobles, including Christopher Seton, were hanged at Newcastle without a trial.

Bruce's rule was at an ebb, and many of his supporters were discouraged. He attempted to enlist men for his small army at Athol.

In August 1306, Bruce and his party camped on land belonging to John of Lorne, a distant Comyn relative. John of Lorne had heard that Bruce was in the area and had asked his tenants to watch for him and his men. Bruce's party was surprised by John of Lorne's men, and the King of Scotland was defeated again. Many of Bruce's party dispersed to avoid capture.

With a small following, Bruce "took to the heather," sleeping in caves and eating only a mixture of raw oatmeal and water, called drammock. After crossing Loch Lomond to Castle Donaverty, Bruce and his men traveled among the Islands of Kintyre and the Hebrides, participating in several forays and skirmishes along the way. They wintered on the Island of Rathlin off the coast of Ireland. The Irish natives didn't provide aid to the refugee Scots but, because they were also hostile to the English, didn't betray them to King Edward's forces.

According to a story passed down from generation to generation, the incident of the spider occurred at Rathlin. Bruce thought that his problems might be due to his killing the Red Comyn in the church at Dumfries, and he considered performing an act of contrition for this great sin. He thought about abandoning his quest to free Scotland from English rule to crusade in the Holy Land against the Saracens. However, he didn't want to shirk his duty as King of Scotland to free his country of the English invaders. He was torn between performing his duty to Scotland and atoning for his past sins. According to Sir Walter Scott in "History of Scotland" from *Tales of a Grandfather*:

> While he was divided twixt these reflections, and doubtful of what he would do, Bruce was looking upward toward the roof of the cabin in which he lay; and his eye was attracted by a spider which, hanging at the end of a long thread of its own spinning, was endeavoring, in the fashion of that creature, to swing itself from one beam in the roof to another, for the purpose of fixing the line on which it meant to stretch its web.

The insect made the attempt again and again without success, and at length Bruce counted that it had tried to carry its point six times, and been as often unable to do so. It came to his head that he had himself fought just six battles against the English and their allies and that the poor persevering spider was exactly in the same situation as himself, having made as many trials, and had been as often disappointed in what he had aimed at.

"Now," thought Bruce, "as I have no means of knowing what is best to be done, I shall be guided by the luck which guides this spider. If the spider shall make another effort to fix its thread and shall be successful, I will venture a seventh time to try my fortune in Scotland; but if the spider shall fail, I will go to the wars in Palestine, and never return to my home country more."

While Bruce was forming his resolution, the spider made another exertion with all the force it could muster, and fairly succeeded in fastening its thread to the beam which it had so often in vain attempted to reach. Bruce, seeing the success of the spider, resolved to try his own fortune; and as he had never before gained a victory, so he never afterward sustained any considerable or decisive check or defeat.

Bruce defeated the English decisively at Bannockburn in June 1314 and finally, in 1328, achieved his goal, the formal recognition of the independence of Scotland by the English Parliament.

JOHN PAUL JONES (1747-1792) Victor Over the *HMS Serapis*

"The conditions of conquest are always easy. We have but to toil
  awhile, endure awhile, believe always, and never turn back."

William Gilmore Simms

In September 1779, during the Revolutionary War, American
Commodore John Paul Jones's squadron patrolled the Yorkshire
coast of England. His mixed crew, which included Arabs, Malays,
Maltese, and Portuguese, had signed up to fight. He had American
officers, but his ship had been commissioned in France, and he had
not been permitted to recruit French sailors. Benjamin Franklin, the
U.S. Minister to France, had helped to obtain the ships for
Commodore Jones's squadron. The East Indiaman *Duras* was
renamed *Bonhomme Richard* in honor of Franklin's *Poor Richard's
Almanac*.

Jones raided Newcastle-on-Tyne to intercept the winter's supply
of coal en route to London. He had four ships: his flagship
Bonhomme Richard with forty worn out guns that had been
scrapped by the French Navy, the frigate *Alliance*, the frigate
Pallas, and the cutter *Vengeance*.

While sailing off Flambough Head on September 23, 1779,
Jones saw a fleet of forty-one sails rounding the Head and
approaching his small squadron. The English pilot on the *Richard*,
who had come aboard thinking she was a Royal Navy ship, told
Jones that this Baltic convoy was escorted by the frigate *Serapis*
(44 guns) and the sloop of war *Countess of Scarborough* (20 guns).

The *HMS Serapis*, commanded by Captain Richard Pearson,
Royal Navy, was rated at 44 guns but actually had 50: 20 eighteen-
pounders on the lower gun deck (vs. *Richard's* 6 eighteen-
pounders), 20 nine-pounders on the upper gun deck (vs. *Richard's*
28 twelve-pounders), and 10 six-pounders on the quarterdeck (vs.
Richard's 6 nine-pounders). Captain Pearson knew that Jones's
squadron was in the area; the bailiffs of Scarborough had sent out
a boat to warn him of the danger.

At 6:00 p.m., Jones made the signal, "Form line of battle," but
the other captains in his squadron ignored it. *Alliance* dropped

back, leaving *Richard* to engage *Serapis*; *Pallas* veered off but later returned and engaged the *Countess of Scarborough*, and *Vengeance* sailed away and looked on from a distance. At 6:30 p.m., *Richard* rounded the port quarter of *Serapis*, and the ships sailed west on the port tack alongside each other.

Captain Pearson asked the *Richard* to identify herself. Jones directed Master Stacey to respond that they were the *Princess Royal*. Pearson asked where they were from. Jones, who was flying the British flag, hesitated in responding. Pearson demanded a response; otherwise he would commence firing. Jones replaced his British colors with the American ensign and commanded his starboard batteries to fire. Simultaneously, Pearson ordered his batteries to fire. Two of Jones's old eighteen-pounders burst when they were fired, destroying the battery as well as the deck above the guns and killing many men.

Each captain attempted to place his ship across the other's bow or stern to use a raking pattern of fire. Pearson, having the faster ship, was more successful in maneuvering. After absorbing several broadsides, Jones realized that he would lose a broadside-to-broadside duel. His only hope was to grapple and board. He dropped astern of the *Serapis*, ran up on her starboard side and attempted to board. His men were repulsed. Next, Pearson tried to place his ship across *Richard's* bow to rake her. He failed, but the relative position of the two ships allowed Jones to run *Richard's* bow into the stern of *Serapis*. Captain Pearson asked Jones if his ship had struck the flag and surrendered. Jones responded with the well-known reply, "I have not yet begun to fight."

Jones was unable to bring any of his cannon to bear on the *Serapis*. He tried to get clear and position the *Richard* across the bow of *Serapis*; he almost succeeded. However, the tip of the bowsprit of the *Serapis* became entangled in the support rigging of the *Richard's* mizzen mast. The wind caused both ships to swing around, causing the fluke of *Serapis's* starboard anchor to pierce the bulwarks of the starboard quarter of the *Richard*. The resulting side by side linkage of the two ships was exactly what Jones wanted.

Captain Pearson tried valiantly to separate the two ships to take advantage of his ship's superior fire power. He ordered *Richard's* grappling hooks to be thrown back or their lines cut. However, twenty French Marines commanded by de Chamillard were positioned on the poop deck of the *Richard* and picked off any *Serapis* hands who attempted this. Captain Pearson also tried dropping his anchor, hoping that the tide and the wind would force the ships apart. This, too, was unsuccessful. The ships were so close that their gun muzzles were touching. The starboard gun ports on the *Serapis*, which had been closed early in the battle when the port guns were firing, couldn't be opened and had to be shot open. *Richard's* gunners had to push their staves into *Serapis's* gun ports to load and to ram their charges into their own gun barrels.

Sails on both ships were on fire on several occasions. Crews stopped the battle to perform damage control functions. By 8:30 p.m., the *Richard* was in bad shape. Jones couldn't use his eighteen-pounders for fear that they would blow up, and his main battery of twelve-pounders had been blasted by *Serapis's* two decks of eighteen-pounders. The only cannons that Jones could bring to bear were three of the six nine-pounders on the quarterdeck. He helped to move one of these to the port side and fired it himself. Jones had the advantage of the excellent marksmanship of the French Marines and of the gunners posted on his masts.

While the two antagonists remained locked together in battle, the *Pallas* continued to engage the *Countess of Scarborough*. On the other hand, Captain Landais in the *Alliance* proved to be a disloyal member of Jones's squadron. When the *Serapis* and the *Richard* became linked together, Landais sailed by and raked the *Richard*, killing two men and driving others from their battle stations. About two hours later, he fired a broadside into the port quarter of the *Richard* that included shots below the water line. His third broadside into the *Richard* took a greater toll when he fired into the forecastle where men who had been driven from their battle stations had gathered. This time he caused many casualties and several fatalities, including a chief petty officer.

In later testimony, Landais claimed that his broadsides forced Captain Pearson to strike his colors and surrender. Of course, it was to Captain Pearson's advantage to claim that he was beaten by two frigates, not one. These attacks on the *Richard* by a member of her own squadron were not accidental. The battle scene was illuminated by a nearly full moon, and the *Richard* had her night recognition signals burning. Also, the upper decks of the *Richard* were painted black; the topsides of the *Serapis* were painted yellow. After the battle, Landais told a French colonel that he intended to help the

Serapis sink the *Richard* and then to board and capture the *Serapis,* thus emerging as the hero of the battle.

Jones continued personally to fire one of the remaining nine-pounders on his quarterdeck since Purser Mease, the officer in charge of the battery of nine-pounders, had received a bad head wound. At one point, a sailor came up to Jones and pleaded with him to strike. Jones responded that he would never strike and went back to firing the nine-pounder. Eventually, Jones's sharpshooters on deck and in the tops picked off so many of the *Serapis's* gunners that the boys bringing up powder cartridges from the magazines could find no one to give them to. They just left the cartridges on the deck.

William Hamilton, a Scottish seaman in Jones's crew, carried a basket of hand grenades up to a yardarm that was directly over an open hatch on the *Serapis*. He dropped a grenade through the hatch, exploding the powder cartridges that the boy "powder monkeys" had left lying on deck. Twenty men were killed, and many were badly burned. Jones loaded his three remaining nine-pounders with double shot to fire at the mainmast of the *Serapis*.

Captain Pearson seriously considered surrendering after the explosion. On the *Richard*, three petty officers decided that the *Richard* would sink if she didn't strike. One of them, Chief Gunner Henry Gardner, ran aft to haul down the ensign to surrender, but found that the flagstaff with the ensign had been shot away. He pleaded with Jones to surrender.

Captain Pearson heard Gardner's pleas and asked Jones if he was asking for quarter. Jones answered, "No sir, I haven't as yet thought of it, but I'm determined to make you strike." Captain Pearson responding by ordering "Boarders away." However, his boarders were repulsed; they returned to the *Serapis* immediately.

At 10:00 p.m., *Richard's* Master at Arms released about one hundred men in the hold from ships that had been captured earlier. They were told to man the pumps if they wanted to survive. One of the prisoners, the Master of the prize ship *Union*, escaped through an open gun port on the *Serapis*. He told Captain Pearson that the *Richard* had five feet of water in her hold and was sinking.

The situation was grim. The *Richard* had sporadic fires in multiple locations and holes below the water line. Jones's officers were weary; his chief petty officers were asking for quarter. He had only three nine-pounders in service and was receiving fire from four eighteen-pounders into his side.

At 10:30 p.m., Jones's double-loaded shot brought down the mainmast of the *Serapis*. Captain Pearson surrendered. He personally had to tear down the ensign, which was nailed to its staff; everyone around him was either dead or wounded. Lieutenant Dale of the *Richard* went aboard the *Serapis* to take possession and to escort Captain Pearson to the *Richard* to introduce him to Commodore Jones. Captain Pearson presented his sword to Jones, who returned it with comments on the gallantry of the *Serapis's* defenders. Jones invited the defeated captain to his cabin for a ceremonial glass of wine.

The battle had lasted about four hours. The *Richard* was in terrible condition. Her transom was almost entirely shot away, and her quarterdeck was about to fall into the gunroom below it. Her upper decks had gaping holes, and the timbers aft of the mainmast on her lower deck were "mangled beyond my power of description," according to Jones.

Commodore John Paul Jones's courage and perseverance in not giving up, when all indications suggested it, were the significant factors in this battle. He certainly displayed his leadership qualities in achieving victory despite overwhelming odds.

HORATIO NELSON (1758-1805) Victor at the Nile, Copenhagen, and Trafalgar

"Wherever the British sailor goes, he carries on the collar of his uniform a memorial of the three great triumphs of his country's greatest admiral, Nelson. But it would not matter if those stripes for the Nile, Copenhagen, and Trafalgar were there or not; the British sailor and all that he stands for is Nelson's monument. The man who smashed Napoleon by sea, who established Britain finally as the undisputed mistress of the seas, whose courage and whose genius were lavishly poured out for the benefit of his country, was indeed worthy of the national sentiment that has made him the greatest of England's heroes."

John Allen, ed., *One Hundred Great Lives*

One of Admiral Lord Horatio Nelson's mentors, Captain William Cornwallis, advised him, "When in doubt, to fight is to err on the right side." Later, Nelson advised his captains, "No captain can do very wrong if he places his ship alongside that of an enemy." Nelson always advocated attack, even when he was outgunned or was at a strategic disadvantage such as at Copenhagen, where he was opposed by Danish forces that could replace their casualties. He was determined to win even if it was by no more than refusing to admit defeat.

In 1793, war broke out between England and France. Nelson participated in a raid on the French garrison at Calvi in Corsica. A shot struck the ground near him and forced sand and small particles of gravel into his right eye. He described it as a "little hurt"; however, he never regained sight in the eye.

In 1797, Nelson participated in his first full-scale naval battle at Cape St. Vincent off the coast of Portugal. Nelson engaged seven Spanish ships of the line with his ship, the *HMS Captain*, and distinguished himself during the battle. He was promoted to rear admiral and was given the Order of the Bath.

Nelson's next action was the interception of Spanish treasure ships attempting to enter Santa Cruz, the harbor of Tenerife. Nelson's men attacked the harbor at Santa Cruz and were met with heavy fire from the fort and nearby houses. After one English captain was killed and another was wounded, Nelson came ashore to take personal command. As he was getting out of his boat, he was hit with grapeshot in the right elbow. The bone was shattered, and the arm had to be amputated.

The Battle of the Nile

In March 1798, during Britain's long and painful war with France, Nelson left England in his flagship, *Vanguard,* bound for the Mediterranean. With him sailed Captain Troubridge in *Culloden,* Captain Foley in *Goliath,* Captain Hood in *Zealous,* and Captain Miller in *Theseus* in a squadron that would later go into battle with fourteen ships. Lord St. Vincent, the commander-in-chief, was pleased to welcome the aggressive Nelson, whose arrival gave his commander "new life."

Napoleon wanted to attack England, but he realized that the French Navy was no match for the Royal Navy. Instead, he carried the war to the Mediterranean by attacking and sacking Malta, which was defended by the Knights of St. John, a shadow of their former strength when they had fought in Palestine during the Crusades. Napoleon, who was General of France's Army and Admiral (assisted by Admiral De Brueys) of France's Navy, loaded Malta's treasures on his flagship, *L'Orient,* and sailed for Egypt.

Nelson arrived in Egypt, but because he was short of frigates, the eyes of the fleet, he did not know the location of the French fleet. Napoleon off-loaded his army from his ships at Marabout. Nelson had used the time looking for Napoleon to train his already highly trained fleet. British seamen may not have been well paid, well fed, or well treated, but they were well trained and when they were asked to fight, they fought well. England was justifiably proud of their "hearts of oak."

The French fleet of seventeen ships, which included the flagship (120 guns), three ships of the line (80 guns each) and nine ships of the line (74 guns each), and four frigates (two with 40 guns and two with 36), outmanned Nelson's ships. Nelson had fourteen ships of the line, all with 74 guns except the smaller *Leander,* and no frigates. The difference in weight of metal was significant; a French seventy-four carried heavier guns than a British seventy-four. However, the level of discipline and training was much higher in the British ships.

Admiral De Brueys had anchored at Aboukir Bay, near the mouth of the Nile, because of excessive silt in the bay at Alexandria. De Brueys felt secure because he had shoals on one side of his ships, breakers on the other side, and his frigates positioned on the flanks. Furthermore, French artillery on Bequier Island provided additional cover for his ships, and sunset was only a few hours away when the British fleet was sighted.

Nelson, who had been restless while searching for the French fleet, was eager for a fight. He said, "Before this time tomorrow, I shall have gained a peerage, or Westminster Abbey." Nelson took a substantial risk by attacking a fleet anchored so close to shore; he assumed that the typically conservative French fleet would not risk anchoring too close to the shoreline.

The battle began at 6:30 p.m., at sundown. Early in the battle, Captain Troubridge's *Culloden* went aground. Each of Nelson's ships mounted four lights in a line at the top of the mizzen mast to distinguish them from French ships. Realizing that he was facing an enemy with superior firepower, Nelson's plan of battle was to bring an overpowering force to bear on part of the French line (the van).

Captain Foley, the most experienced of Nelson's captains, in *Goliath,* took the initiative by leading *Zealous, Theseus, Orion,* and *Audacious* between the first ship in the French line, *Le Guerrier,* and the French battery on Bequier Island to position themselves between the shoreline and the French line of ships. These ships brought concentrated fire to bear on the French line, destroying the French ships in the van within two hours of the start of the battle. Captain Darby's ship, *Bellerophon,* had her masts and cables shot away by *L'Orient* and drifted out of control. *Majestic* had many casualties; her Captain, Westcott, was killed.

Admiral De Brueys in *L'Orient* fought on after receiving three wounds, two in the body and one in the head, before being cut in two by the fourth shot. Commodore Casabianca assumed command until *L'Orient,* with all of Malta's treasures, blew up at ten o'clock. The explosion was heard at Alexandria, fifteen miles away.

During the battle, Nelson was struck in the forehead by a piece of iron shot, causing a flap of skin to hang down over his right eye, his blind eye. The three-inch wound in his forehead, which bared his skull, bled profusely, and he was temporarily blinded. Although he was in great pain, when the doctor left the sailor he was treating to attend the admiral, Nelson said, "No, I will take my turn with my brave fellows."

Nelson drafted a report of the battle for Lord St. Vincent and the Lord Commissioners of the Admiralty:

> Nothing could withstand the squadron your Lordships did me the honor to place under my command. Their high state of discipline is well known to you, and with the judgment of the captains, together with their valor, and that of officers and men of every description, it was absolutely irresistible. Could anything from my pen add to the character of the captains I would write it with pleasure, but that is impossible.

Lord Howe wrote to Nelson that he thought it notable that *every* captain had done his duty. Howe had experienced naval battles in which that statement could not have been made. Nelson felt that he owed a description of the battle to Howe, whom he thought was the "first and greatest sea-officer the world has ever produced." "I had the happiness to command a Band of Brothers. Each knew his duty, and I was sure each would feel for a French ship. By attacking the enemy's van and center, the wind blowing directly along their line, I was enabled to throw what force I pleased on a few ships. We always kept a superior force to the enemy."

Of the seventeen ships in Admiral De Bruey's fleet, all but four were either on fire or flying the British Union Jack the next morning. Nelson had not lost a single ship; it was the most complete victory that the Royal Navy had ever experienced. The French had six times the casualties, 5225, of the British, including men who were missing or captured. The Admiralty, which had been criticized for choosing a young admiral like Nelson for such an important command, was justified in its choice. England was overjoyed with Nelson's victory; he was raised to the peerage with the title Baron Nelson of the Nile.

Battle of Copenhagen

In 1801, Admiral Nelson embarked to the Baltic with a fleet under the command of Admiral Sir Hyde Parker. Denmark, Sweden, and Russia had joined in an alliance against England called the League of Neutrality because England, during the war with France, had interfered with their shipping. The League of Neutrality was a stance of armed neutrality in which England was denied the right of "visit and search" that they had always demanded. Russia was the leader of the league, and Emperor Paul I of Russia had imposed an embargo on English shipping in his ports. Also, France pressured Denmark and Sweden to use their navies against England.

Nelson wanted to attack the Russian port of Reval. However, he was second-in-command to Sir Hyde Parker, an elderly, conservative admiral close to retirement who didn't want healthy Danish and Swedish fleets between him and England. The English had a choice of attacking these potential enemies before they assumed the initiative or relying on the presence of a large Royal Navy fleet and using threatening language to subdue the League.

The British decided to destroy the Danish fleet at Copenhagen. Earlier attempts to negotiate with the Danes had merely given the Danes more time to prepare for battle. Nelson suggested that they strike at once. Admiral Parker's hesitation was understandable; the Danes had fortified Copenhagen harbor heavily.

The harbor couldn't be approached from the North because of the Trekroner (three crowns) fort with over seventy guns. South of the fort, the Danes had dismasted and moored eighteen men-of-war with a total of 634 guns in a line one and a half miles in length along the inner or King's Channel. Immediately in front of the harbor was the Middle Ground, a shoal that prevented a straight-in approach. The English would have to enter the harbor in a single file but couldn't use their heavy ships, which had too much draft to negotiate the channel.

Only the light ships of the line, along with frigates, could be used in the harbor; Admiral Parker, with the heavy ships of the line, positioned himself to prevent any Swedish or Russian ships from coming to the aid of the Danes. To make navigation by the enemy difficult, the Danes had removed all of the buoys from the channel. Soundings were taken, and the buoys were replaced under the personal supervision of Admiral Nelson during the evening before the battle.

Nelson shifted his flag from his flagship, the *St. George*, to the lighter *Elephant* (74 guns) commanded by Captain Foley, who had led the line at the Battle of the Nile. In Nelson's plan of battle, twelve ships of the line would fight in the harbor while the frigates, under Captain Riou, would be held in reserve.

The battle started badly for the British, when the second ship of the line, *Agamemnon*, went aground on the Middle Ground Shoal. Two other ships of the line, the *Bellona* and the *Russell*, went aground attempting to maneuver around the shoal.

The nine ships that made it into position provided cover for the three ships that went aground. Initially, neither the end of the Danish line nor the Danish fort had any opposition. Captain Riou attempted to take on the end of the Danish line with his frigates and was met with extremely heavy fire. The Danes had the advantage of being able to row men out to the hulks to replace those who were killed or wounded.

The guns of Admiral Parker's ships were out of range and could not help Nelson's ships. Parker could see that Nelson was taking a pounding; the Danes' fire was more accurate than anticipated.

The Danes proved to be tough opponents. Finally, Admiral Parker decided to discontinue the action. He sent his flag captain, Captain Otway, to go aboard Nelson's ship, *Elephant*, to find out what was happening.

Before Captain Otway could report back to Sir Hyde, the Commander-in-chief flew signal number thirty-nine to leave off action. Nelson continued flying signal number sixteen, the signal for close action. Nelson looked at Parker's signal to leave off action, turned to Captain Foley, captain of the *Elephant*, and said, "You know Foley, I only have one eye. I have a right to be blind sometimes." Then he raised his telescope to his right eye, his blind eye, and said, "I really do not see the signal."

After five hours of heated conflict, a truce was granted, and both sides tended their wounded. The casualties were heavy; however, the Danish casualties were many times the English casualties of just under a thousand men. Truce negotiations dragged on, but, finally, the Battle of Copenhagen was declared an important victory for the English. The battle was won because Nelson refused to stop fighting and admit defeat.

The Battle of Trafalgar

In the fall of 1805, Nelson prepared for what would be his last battle. Under his command were twenty-seven ships of the line, four frigates, a schooner, and a cutter. His squadron included Admiral Collingwood (his second in command) in *Royal Sovereign,* Captain Berry in *Agamemnon*, Captain Harvey in *Téméraire*, and Captain Freemantle in *Neptune*. Captain Hardy, Nelson's friend, commanded *Victory,* his flagship.

Admiral Villeneuve, in command of the combined French and Spanish fleet at Trafalgar, instructed the captains under his command of Nelson's intentions: "He will try to double our rear, cut through the line, and bring against the ships thus isolated groups of his own, to surround and capture them. Captains must rely on their courage and love of glory, rather than the signals of the Admiral, who may already be engaged and wrapped in smoke. The captain who is not in action is not at his post." Nelson's written instructions to his captains were similar to what Villeneuve had expected:

> The order of sailing was to be the order of battle. The second in command, Admiral Collingwood, after Nelson's intentions had been made known by signal, would have entire direction of the line. If possible he was to cut through the enemy about the twelfth ship from the rear. The remainder of the combined fleet was to be left to the management of the commander-in-chief, whose endeavor would be to see that, while the rear was pulverized by Collingwood, no interference should be encountered from the van.

Villeneuve commanded thirty-three ships of the line (eighteen French and fifteen Spanish), five French frigates, and two brigs. During the evening of October 19, the brig *Argus* notified Villeneuve on the French flagship, *Bucentaure,* that eighteen British ships had been sighted.

Prior to going into battle, Nelson thought of his family. He wrote a document asking his country to provide for his beloved wife Emma Hamilton "that they will give her an ample provision to maintain her rank in life," and he also left "to the beneficence of my country my adopted daughter, Horatia."

At six o'clock the next morning, Nelson signaled his fleet from his flagship, *Victory,* to form into two columns while sailing toward the combined French and Spanish fleets. Nelson's officers on the *Victory* convinced him that the flagship should not be the first ship to go into action. He seemed to agree to let *Téméraire* go into action ahead of *Victory;* however, *Victory* did not give way, and Nelson hailed *Téméraire* from the quarterdeck, "I'll thank you, Captain Harvey, to keep your proper station, which is astern of *Victory*."

Nelson signalled his squadron, "England expects that every man will do his duty," followed by the signal for close action. Collingwood in *Royal Sovereign* went into action well ahead of his squadron, cutting the line of the combined fleet just astern of the *Santa Anna,* Admiral Alava's flagship.

Gunfire from the topmasts of the combined fleets' *Redoubtable* rained down on the deck of *Victory* until *Téméraire* came up to support *Victory.* At 1:15 p.m., Hardy saw Nelson, on his knees, fall to the deck. He told Hardy, "They have done for me at last, Hardy." A shot from the fighting tops of *Redoubtable* had shattered Nelson's left shoulder, penetrated his chest, and lodged in his spine.

Nelson was carried below. Hardy visited Nelson to give him status of the battle: "We have got twelve or fourteen of the enemy's ships in our possession but five of their van have tacked, and show an intention of bearing down on *Victory*. I have therefore called two or three of our fresh ships around us, and we are giving them a drubbing."

Hardy returned to his duty station to send Collingwood a message about the severity of Nelson's wound. He visited Nelson about an hour later. Nelson asked Hardy to "take care of my dear Lady Hamilton, Hardy; take care of poor Lady Hamilton. Kiss me, Hardy." After Hardy had kissed his cheek, Nelson said, "Now I am satisfied. Thank God, I have done my duty." Before returning to the deck, Hardy bent down again and kissed his dying friend on the forehead. Nelson died at 4:30 p.m.

Nelson had won another overwhelming victory. Villeneuve was a prisoner, his combined fleet was scattered, and no British ships had been lost. Nelson was mourned by an appreciative nation. His body was shipped home and on December 23 was transported up the Thames River to Greenwich, where it lay in state in Christopher Wren's Painted Hall in a coffin made from timber from *L'Orient*. The body was taken to Whitehall and the Admiralty and finally to St. Paul's Cathedral for burial.

DUKE OF WELLINGTON (1769-1852) Defeated Napoleon at Waterloo

"Hard pounding this, gentlemen; let's see who will pound the longest."

Duke of Wellington at Waterloo

In April 1815, just prior to the Battle of Waterloo, George Canning said to Lord Castlereagh, "what a happy consummation of his [Wellington's] story it would be to put the last hand to the destruction of Bonaparte's power in direct conflict with Bonaparte." Wellington did, and it was.

On April 5, 1815, the Duke of Wellington assumed command in Brussels, Belgium, of the joint forces of Great Britain and the Netherlands. His mission, with these joint forces and a Prussian Army, was to perform advance guard duties until they could be joined by armies from Austria and Russia.

The British contingent of his army was comprised of six cavalry regiments and twenty-five infantry battalions, approximately 14,000 men. Half of these men had never been in battle. Most of Wellington's Peninsular Army, which had fought in Portugal and Spain, had been demobilized. Many of those who hadn't been demobilized had fought in the War of 1812 in the United States or were en route from there. The other half of his army was made up of combined Dutch and Belgian forces who were less experienced and less dependable than his British contingent.

Wellington's forces expanded to 60,000 by the end of April and to 90,000 by mid-June. He organized his army into three corps and strengthened his green units by placing British or King's German Legion troops alongside inexperienced men. Wellington and General Blucher, commander of the Prussian Army, defended a front that extended over one hundred miles, from Liege to Tournai. Apprehension of attack by Napoleon diminished as the Allied Army added units. The Prussian Army grew to approximately 113,000 by mid-June, but was spread out from Charleroi to the Ardennes Forest; the smaller British-Netherlands-German Legion Army manned the frontier from the North Sea to Mons.

On the evening of June 15, the Duchess of Richmond gave a ball in Brussels that was attended by most senior officers of the Allied

Armies, including the Duke of Wellington and the Prince of Orange, who commanded the Netherlands contingent. Wellington had insisted on attending the ball in an attempt to prevent civilians from fleeing the Belgian capital in panic.

Several times during the evening, Wellington received messages and wrote and sent orders. Many of his staff left the ball early, reacting to the news that at dawn that morning Napoleon with approximately 124,000 men had crossed the Sambre River and attacked the right wing of Blucher's army near where it joined the left wing of Wellington's army.

The initial communication from Blucher that had been received in mid-afternoon was sketchy and no longer current. Wellington couldn't commit the bulk of his forces until he knew which of three roads to Brussels—through Charleroi, through Mons, or through Tournai—Napoleon was going to use. Before he left the ball, Wellington had heard that the attack on the Prussians was a serious one, and he ordered a concentration of his forces at Quatre-Bras near Nivelles, several miles west of the Charleroi-Brussels road.

By mid-afternoon on Friday, June 16, the left wing of Napoleon's army, commanded by Marshal Ney, almost over-whelmed the forces of the Prince of Orange at Quatre-Bras. During the afternoon, one British division unsupported by cavalry held off three of Ney's divisions with 4,000 cavalrymen.

Wellington personally directed the defense; he issued tactical orders to every battalion and even to selected companies. He was an energetic general in the prime of his life and an active participant in the action.

While trying to rally a light cavalry unit, Wellington was surrounded by French lancers. He escaped by jumping his chestnut horse, Copenhagen, a veteran of the Peninsular Campaign, over a ditch filled with infantry, bayonets and all. Eventually, when additional allied troops joined the battle, Wellington took the offensive and drove back Ney's forces. However, Wellington's ally, Blucher, with 80,000 Prussians, was beaten back at Ligny by 63,000 seasoned French troops. In another close call, Blucher was almost captured by the French cavalry when they overran his position.

Napoleon detached a force of 33,000 under Marshal Grouchy to pursue the Prussians as they withdrew northward toward Wavre. Napoleon's directive to Grouchy was contradictory. In an earlier communication, Grouchy had indicated his intention of pursuing the Prussians to separate them from Wellington's army. However, Napoleon's orders were: "His Majesty desires you will head for Wavre in order to draw near to us." The portion of the message with which Grouchy complied was the order, "head for Wavre." This virtually ensured that these 33,000 men wouldn't be available to Napoleon at Waterloo.

During Saturday morning, Napoleon pressured Wellington, who withdrew in an orderly fashion to the ridge of Mont St. Jean, twelve miles south of Brussels. Wellington maintained communications with his Prussian Allies, who were only twelve miles to the east. Wellington knew well the ridge to which he had retired; he had studied it as a potential site for a battle. The ridge had places to conceal his troops on the reverse slopes and a forest behind them extended for miles, providing a refuge for his green troops if they needed it. Wellington had to maintain a defensive position, since he couldn't do complicated maneuvers with his relatively untrained troops.

Wellington realized that coordination of his combined army and the Prussian Army was crucial. Together they could defeat Napoleon; separately they couldn't. Wellington continued to sprinkle seasoned British and German Legion troops throughout his less seasoned units. He employed his less dependable units and those units with heavy casualties as guards for his flanks and as reserves. Wellington located his principal reserve behind his right flank to the west under the command of his most reliable corps commander, General "Daddy" Hill.

Wellington placed his main force on the reverse slope of the hill and positioned his artillery, which had smaller and fewer cannons than the French, along the ridge. Then he hid his skirmishers in the cornfields on the forward slope of the hill, ensuring that the French would have to move through three lines of fire. Wellington had several units, including General Clinton's 2nd [Infantry] Division, that were extremely maneuverable and operated like light infantry divisions. He maintained good communications and moved units quickly to the weak points.

Napoleon was confident of victory that day, as he had been against the Prussians with their superior numbers on the previous day. He was sure that many of Wellington's less well-trained units would break and run when confronted with his veterans. Napoleon outlined his plan of battle: "I shall hammer them with my artillery, charge them with my cavalry to make them show themselves, and, when I am quite sure where the actual English are, I shall go straight at them with my Old Guard."

On Sunday, June 18, around noon, Napoleon opened the fighting with a feint at Hougoumont to the east. Prince Jerome's French troops were beaten back; a second diversion was made at the same location with a larger body of troops. Then Prince Jerome attempted to take Hougoumont a third time. Wellington held on by dispatching four companies of the Life Guards to enforce the position.

The feint at Hougoumont was the first phase of the Battle of Waterloo. Napoleon massed the main body of his troops at the center, where he planned his principal attack. When the French bombardment began, Napoleon observed troop movements about five or six miles away toward Wavre. At first he thought they were Grouchy's troops sent to pursue the Prussians. Then he realized what Wellington already knew; they were Blucher's troops hurrying to rejoin Wellington. Napoleon decided to make a frontal attack on the center. He would deal with Wellington first, then with Blucher. He sent reserves to delay the Prussians.

The second phase of the battle began at one o'clock when the French began a bombardment with eighty guns, including twenty-four of the dreaded twelve-pounders. The cannonade was intense, but it inflicted minimal casualties due to Wellington's disposition of the men on the reverse slope of the ridge.

At 1:30 p.m., Count D'Erlon ordered the French right to attack. The grenadiers attacked to the beating of drums in a formation of four hundred shouting men abreast. They were met, but not stopped, by Wellington's artillery. The French overran and isolated the Germans defending La Haye Sainte, who were driven from their position in an orchard. The fighting at the crest of the ridge was critical. Sir Thomas Picton's division was ordered to advance to meet D'Erlon's attack. Picton's division was led by his Peninsular commanders, Pack and Kempt, and was made up of veterans. Sir Dennis Pack ordered the Gordons, the Blackwatch, and the 44th forward; Sir Thomas Picton led Kempt's line personally, until a bullet pierced the top hat that he wore in battle and struck him in the temple. He was killed instantly.

Wellington ordered Lord Uxbridge to charge with the Household and Union Brigades of heavy cavalry, under Lord Edward Somerset on the right and Sir William Ponsonby on the left. The Union Brigade was composed of the Royal Dragoons, the Scots Greys, and the Inniskillings from Ireland. Wellington personally led the Life Guards in the advance. Wellington's heavy cavalry carried away everything in its path. The awe-inspiring charge routed a sizable body of French infantry in formation. However, Uxbridge was unable to control the charge. The cavalry overran its positions, and then went on the defensive with substantial loss of life. The heavy cavalry wasn't an effective fighting force for the remainder of the battle. Wellington lost 2,500 cavalrymen in this charge, about one quarter of those available to him.

The third phase of the battle began with an act of poor judgement by Marshal Ney. He decided that taking the central section of the ridge was his responsibility, and that he would do it with cavalry alone. Napoleon's cavalry was nearly as numerous as the British infantry. Wellington was astounded to see the French heavy cavalry, one of the world's finest, forming up to advance upon the allied infantry without infantry support.

Wellington ordered his 1st and 3rd divisions opposite the point of attack to form battalion squares in a checkerboard fashion, such that the front edge of each square had a clear field of fire with respect to the next square. He ordered his men to lie down in the cornfields on the plateau until the French cavalry came within range. Between the squares, Wellington placed his last two reserve batteries of Horse Artillery. Their nine-pounders were filled with double loads of anti-personnel grapeshot. Behind the squares, he placed his cavalry, including the remnants of the two brigades of heavy cavalry that Lord Uxbridge had been unable to control.

The French cavalry came at the Allied squares in formation at a controlled pace. The British artillery caused havoc along the line of advancing cavalry; horses were down all over the central portion of the plateau. The allied infantry held their fire and then fired upon order in unison. The results were devastating. Ney varied the attack, but the British and Hanover infantry remained cool and unyielding. The French cavalry approached the squares from the sides and, at one point, from the rear. Napoleon's cavalry charged the battalion squares five times without success. Wellington may not have been able to maneuver with his relatively inexperienced army, but he could rely on them to hold a position with tenacity under heavy fire.

Although Napoleon and Wellington were both in their mid-forties, Napoleon, unlike Wellington, hadn't played an active role in the battle until this point. Early in the day, Napoleon studied the battlefield and issued orders to his Marshals. Then, in effect, he delegated control of the offensive to Marshal Ney. Napoleon was fatigued from the strenuous activity of the last three days and was suffering from hemorrhoids. He spent several hours of the afternoon lying down at his headquarters at Rossomme in a semi-comatose state. Napoleon roused himself and took over direction of the battle from Ney. He was ready to direct another victory as he had done so many times before. He moved forward to La Belle-Alliance and ordered Ney to take the farm at La Haye Sainte.

The farm at La Haye Sainte was defended by fewer than four hundred men of the King's German Legion commanded by a British officer, Major George Baring. They had started the day with sixty rounds of ammunition per man, but were down to four or five rounds each. Their appeals for more ammunition had gone unheeded. Two light companies were the only reinforcement they received. When their ammunition ran out, they defended the farm with bayonets. The only survivors of La Haye Sainte were Major Baring and forty-two men who fought their way through the French lines with their bayonets.

Just after six o'clock, Ney renewed the attack on the allied center with two columns of infantry and cavalry, which were driven back by the British artillery. Wellington re-formed Clinton's veteran division from the reserve and Chasse's Hollanders from the west behind the center of the line. Also, he reduced the squares to four deep to allow increased firepower against infantry but to retain their effectiveness against the reduced cavalry threat.

The young Prince of Orange was in charge of the center of the line. On two occasions, he had deployed Ompteda's battalions of King's German Legion against cavalry with disastrous results. A breakthrough of the center of the allied line was averted only by a charge of the 3rd Hussars of the German Legion and the accurate firepower of the 1st battalion of the 95th Rifles. Ney noted that the center was vulnerable. He asked Napoleon for more men to exploit the opportunity. Napoleon asked Ney if he expected him to create them. Napoleon had twelve battalions of the Imperial Guard still in reserve, but he wasn't ready to commit everything at this point.

Wellington was aware of the dilemma that confronted him. He assigned every reserve that he could muster to shore up his crumbling center, including five inexperienced Brunswick battalions and Vivian's light cavalry. The artillery fire from both sides was intense. The young Brunswickers began to break, but were rallied by Wellington's personal effort.

Wellington rode up to Sir Alexander Frazer, commander of the Horse Artillery, and said, "Twice have I saved this day by perseverance." Wellington was known to be modest about his abilities. However, Frazer agreed with the observation and noted that Wellington was "cool and indifferent at the beginning of battles but when the moment of difficulty comes, intelligence flashes from the eyes of this wonderful man and he rises superior to all that can be imagined." Lord Uxbridge, Wellington's deputy commander, who hadn't served with him previously, later told Lady Shelley, "I thought I had heard enough of this man but he has far surpassed my expectations. He is not a man but a god."

Napoleon, who was about three-quarters of a mile away from the line, and Wellington could both see Blucher's Prussian 1st Corps commanded by General Zieten about two miles away, hurrying to Wellington's aid. Earlier, Zieten had been informed by a Prussian staff officer that Wellington was withdrawing when he saw the allied army retiring to the ridge. The staff officer ordered the Prussian 1st Corps to retrace their steps and to move toward Blucher. General Muffling told Zieten that the battle would be lost if the 1st Corps didn't go to Wellington's aid. Zieten ordered his Prussians back toward Wellington.

Napoleon, having missed his chance to break the allied center, realized that the moment of crisis had come. He ordered aides to carry the word that the men in the distance were Grouchy's coming to his aid, not Blucher's coming to support Wellington. Shortly after seven o'clock, Napoleon committed his Imperial Guard, and the final phase of the battle began.

Napoleon issued a general order for all units to advance and delegated Ney to lead the attack. The Imperial Guards moved toward the ridge in two columns, one advancing toward the center of the allied right and one climbing between Hougoumont and the center. Wellington placed himself at the point at which the main blow was aimed—to the right of the Life Guards. As he had done previously, he ordered his men to lie down in the corn fields until the Imperial Guard was within rifle range. Wellington's artillery was particularly effective against the front ranks of the Imperial guards and caused many casualties, including many of the Old Guard's seasoned officers. Ney walked up the hill after his fifth mount was shot out from under him.

As he had done earlier with Vivian's cavalry, Wellington placed Vandeleur's cavalry behind some of his less seasoned units, that is, between them and the woods behind them. This created a steadying influence on the younger units. When Wellington gave the order to stand and fire, advance units of the Imperial Guards were only twenty yards away. The results of fifteen hundred men firing at close range was devastating. The Imperial Guards reeled, but they didn't break. They re-formed and returned heavy fire, assisted effectively by the French artillery.

At this point, Colonel John Colbourne, commanding the first battalion of the 52nd, made a maneuver on his own initiative that played a decisive role in the last phase of the battle. He moved his battalion forward about 300 yards in front of the line and, as it encountered the leading units of the advancing French, ordered a pivoting movement to the left, thus facing the flank of the Imperial Guard. Colbourne risked leaving a gap in the line, and he also risked being cut down by the French Cavalry. However, his daring move paid off; the initial fire from the Imperial Guard took down one hundred and forty men of his battalion, but the 52nd's return fire was so effective that the Imperial Guard broke and fled.

Napoleon's Old Guard, which had never been defeated, turned and ran. When the battered remnants of Napoleon's army saw the Imperial Guard in flight, they turned around and joined them. Dusk was near, and Wellington waved his men on to pursue the retreating Frenchmen. He realized that this was the crucial moment of victory. He ordered Vivian's and Vandeleur's cavalry in pursuit, joined by Zieten's Prussian cavalry from the east. The rout was complete; many of Napoleon's men stacked their arms and ran to the rear.

Wellington met his ally, Blucher, at nine o'clock, in the advancing darkness, between LaBelle Alliance and Rossomme, the two sites at which Napoleon had spent most of his day. Blucher greeted his comrade in arms with "Mein lieber comrade." Wellington responded with "Quelle affaire" since he didn't speak German, and he knew that Blucher didn't speak English. His greeting was in the language of the army he had just beaten. Wellington's personal view of his battles was:

> I look upon Salamanca, Vitoria, and Waterloo as my three best battles—those which had great and permanent consequences. Salamanca relieved the whole south of Spain, changed all of the prospects of the war—it was felt even in Prussia; Vitoria freed the Peninsula altogether, broke off the armistice at Dresden and thus led to Leipzig and the deliverance of Europe; and Waterloo did more than any other battle I know toward the true object of all battles—the peace of the world.

MUSTAFA KEMAL (1881-1938) Victor at Gallipoli and Father of Modern Turkey

"The hero in history is the individual to whom we can justifiably attribute preponderant influence in determining an issue or an event whose consequences would have been profoundly different if he [or she] had not acted as he [or she] did."

Sydney Hook, *The Hero in History*

Mustafa Kemal played such a vital role in winning the Battle of Gallipoli that is difficult to think of another military officer who influenced the outcome of a campaign to the extent that he did. He assumed responsibility beyond his rank and kept going without sleep despite bouts of malaria. When he became the leader of modern Turkey, he brought his country reluctantly into the twentieth century by the force of his will.

Before Mustafa Kemal (Atatürk, father of all the Turks), Turkey was the decadent, downtrodden "sick man of Europe," with its mixture of races and religions and its poor and uneducated populace. It was burdened by sultans who ruled as despots, by participation in foreign wars that it could not afford, and by foreign exploitation. Its government was disintegrating, and the past glories of the once-powerful Ottoman Empire were memories.

Kemal virtually dragged Turkey into modern times. When he became President in 1923, he abolished the sultanate and the Islamic caliphate (the Moslem secular and religious head of state), outlawed the Arabic alphabet, installed the Latin alphabet, and emancipated Turkish women. He knew that Turkey would not reach its full potential if women were held down. "Kemal campaigned against ... customs that restricted women, maintaining that if they did not share in the social life of the nation, we shall never attain our full development.'"

He encouraged western dress, passed a law that forbade Turkish men to wear the fez, and discouraged the wearing of veils in public by women. His reforms were sweeping. He began a movement to elevate national pride and rewrite Turkish history to place less emphasis on past accomplishments of the Ottoman Empire.

Mustafa Kemal's reputation was made defending the Gallipoli Peninsula from the attacking Allies, principally British Commonwealth forces, in early World War I. Lieutenant Colonel Kemal was assigned to command the 19th Division by Enver Pasha, the Minister of War. When he asked about the location of the division, he was referred to the offices of the General Staff; no one seemed to know much about the 19th Division.

Finally, since Turkey was allied with Germany in World War I, it was suggested that he speak with the German Chief of Staff, General Liman von Sanders. The General said that no such division existed, but that the Third Army Corps stationed at Gallipoli might be planning to form the 19th Division. Kemal was advised to go to Gallipoli and ask about the new unit being formed.

In February 1915, the British Army pounded the forts at the entrance to the Dardanelles, and the Royal Navy and supporting French naval units bombarded other defensive locations. The Royal Navy failed to break through the Narrows in March. This attack was not followed up; the British waited until they could support their navy by an attack on land. Enver Pasha assigned General von Sanders to command the Fifth Army defending the Dardanelles. The headquarters of the 19th Division, an element of the Fifth Army, was located at Maidos.

Von Sanders had six divisions in the Fifth Army to cover the fifty-two-mile coastline of the peninsula. His assessment of potential landing spots differed from Kemal's. He assigned two divisions to the field of Troy and two divisions to the northern end of the peninsula at Bulair. Another division was directed to Cape Helles, and Kemal's 19th Division was held in reserve to move to the area of greatest need.

Kemal moved his headquarters to the village of Boghali, within easy reach of both coasts. Kemal thought that the British would land either at Cape Helles at the southern end of the peninsula, where they could use their naval guns most effectively, or at Gaba Tepe on the western coast to allow ease of movement to the Narrows on the eastern coast.

Early in the morning of April 25, 1915, the Allies landed in force at the two locations Kemal had anticipated. The British landed at Cape Helles, and the Australians and New Zealanders landed at Ariburnu, just north of Gaba Tepe. These landings were accompanied by two diversions, a raid by the French on the Asiatic coast and a Royal Naval Division at Bulair. Von Sanders fell for the diversionary maneuver at Bulair and sent a third division to join the two he had already located there.

Kemal was awakened at Boghali that morning by naval guns and found that he was near the center of the action. He sent a cavalry unit to Koja Chemen, a crest on the Sari Bair range, a ridge that ran parallel to the western shoreline. Kemal received a report that a small enemy force was climbing the slope to the Chunuk Bair crest and received a request from the division on his flank to send a battalion to halt their advance. He realized immediately that this was the site of the major offensive. He knew that the Sari Bair ridge, particularly the Chunuk Bair crest, was crucial to the Turkish defense. Kemal ordered his best regiment, the 57th, and a battery of artillery to move to the Chunuk Bair crest.

It was a bold move that committed a significant portion of von Sander's reserve division and exceeded Kemal's authority as a division commander. If he were wrong, and the major offensive was at a different location, only one Turkish regiment would be available to oppose it. However, he was confident that he was right. In fact, he had acted correctly, and the Australians and New Zealanders (Anzacs) landed in force at Ariburnu, which became known as Anzac Cove.

Kemal personally led the 57th regiment up the hill to Chunuk Bair. As they neared the crest, the Turkish unit that had been located there came running down the slope. Kemal asked them why they were running away. They said the English were coming, and they were out of ammunition. He ordered them to fix bayonets and to lie on the ground. The Australian troops, which were closer to the crest than the Turks were, lay down also. Then, as the 57th regiment came up the slope, Kemal ordered them to take the crest and to set up a mountain battery on the highest ground. His orders were, "I don't order you to attack, I order you to die. In the time it takes us to die, other troops and commanders can come and take our places." By the end of the day, most of the 57th regiment had taken his orders literally.

Although the Turks experienced heavy casualties, they prevented the Anzacs from moving off the beaches. During the day, Kemal ordered a second regiment into the line to reinforce the 57th.

Again, he acted without authority, but, as before, he notified the corps commander, Essad Pasha, of his actions. He urged Essad Pasha to commit the last regiment of the 19th division to defend the Sari Bair front. Essad agreed, gave him the remaining regiment, and, in effect, put him in charge of the entire Sari Bair front. General von Sanders continued to think that the main Allied attack would be at Bulair and telegraphed that he would not commit any additional troops to the Sari Bair front.

By midnight, General Birdwood, the Anzac commander, requested permission from Sir Ian Hamilton, the British commander-in-chief, to return to the ships. Sir Ian denied them permission to evacuate the beaches and ordered them to dig in. He reasoned that the British forces at Cape Helles had established a beachhead and would take pressure off of the troops at Anzac Cove.

On the morning of April 26, Kemal led the remnants of the 57th regiment and the regiment that reinforced them down the slopes in a attack on the Anzacs. He recklessly exposed himself to fire and had three horses shot out from under him. His reputation as a fearless leader of men was reinforced daily. His orders to his men were: "Every soldier who fights here with me must realize that he is in honor bound not to retreat one step. Let me remind you that if you want to rest, there may be no rest for the whole nation throughout eternity. I am sure that all our comrades agree on this, and that they will show no signs of fatigue until the enemy is finally hurled into the sea." General von Sanders was aware of Kemal's role in the defense of Chunuk Bair. In June, Kemal was promoted to Colonel.

Kemal tried in vain to convince Essad Pasha of the importance of the Ariburnu area in the coming offensive. Essad visited Kemal and was given a personal tour of the defenses. Kemal attempted to persuade Essad that the next attack would be on the beaches along Sulva Bay, up the Sazlidere ravine to Chunuk Bair. Essad disagreed with Kemal. He thought that the terrain was too difficult, and that the Allies would not attempt to move any forces other than small raiding parties through it.

Heavy Allied bombardment continued both from naval guns and shore-based artillery. One day Kemal was sitting on a rocky outcropping calmly smoking a cigarette and talking with his men. An artillery shell landed about one hundred yards away from him. The next shell, obviously from the same battery, burst fifty yards away. The third shell struck twenty yards away, sending pieces of rock flying. His men pleaded with him to take cover, but he remained seated where he was. He said that he did not want to set a bad example for his men. After waiting for the fourth shell, which never came, Kemal observed that there must have been only three guns in that battery.

On August 6, the Allies shifted their main offensive to the Ariburnu front. They planned an assault along the Sari Bair ridge. One advance was planned to go up the Sazlidere ravine to Chunuk Bair, precisely as Kemal had predicted, and a second to attack the Koja Chemen summit. Both of these planned advances were supported by the landing of fresh troops at Sulva Bay. Again, von Sanders expected the main attack to come against Bulair or at the southern end of the Sari Bair range, not at the center where Kemal's forces were located. In fact, the Allies landed a diversionary force at the southern end of the range, which caused Essad Pasha to commit most of his reserves to the wrong location.

Belatedly, von Sanders realized his mistake and ordered units from Bulair and Helles to Anzac Cove and Sulva Bay; however, it took them twenty-four hours to reach their destinations. Allied forces scaled the slopes during the night and attacked at dawn. The attack was ferocious. Allied forces climbed to the crest of Chunuk Bair and found it defended by one machine gun crew—and they were asleep. For some inexplicable reason, the Turkish infantry had left the crest.

Turkish defenders were confused. Kemal was aware from an early stage of the attack of disorder on his right. Casualties mounted. The German commander of the division adjacent to the 19th Division sustained a severe chest wound. Two division commanders of the division holding the ridge were killed, and it was now commanded by a lieutenant colonel who was more experienced in running a railway than directing a battle.

Kemal appealed to von Sanders to place all available forces under a unified command or be faced with catastrophe. He asked to be appointed as commander of the unified forces. Von Sanders had confidence in Kemal's ability. He promoted him to General, which entitled him to be addressed as "Pasha," and appointed him commander of the Anafarta front. Kemal's energy level was incredible. The first three nights of his unified command he went without sleep, even though he suffered from severe bouts of malaria.

The battle became a race for the crest of the Anafarta ridge, particularly the Tekke Tepe summit. The Turks won the race by a half hour. They continued down the other side of the crest once they reached it and inflicted murderous fire on the British forces. In fact, the Turkish fire was so intense that the surrounding brush caught fire. The Sulva offensive was not successful; nevertheless, the Anzacs were still hanging on at Chunuk Bair.

After a fourth night without sleep and while feverish with malaria, Kemal personally led a attack on Chunuk Bair. His instructions to his troops were, "Soldiers, there is no doubt that we are going to defeat the enemy in front of you. But do not hurry. Let me go ahead first. As soon as you see me raise my whip, then you will all leap forward." The Turks overwhelmed the men in front of them and drove them back to the beaches.

Kemal was struck in the chest with a bullet as he led fresh troops from Bulair to drive the Anzacs off Chunuk Bair. He moved his left hand cautiously over the painful spot in his right ribs, but observed no blood. He opened his tunic and found an ugly blue and red bruise about three inches in diameter in his lower right ribs. He reached into the small inner pocket of his tunic and took out the pocket watch that he had carried since military school. The bullet had struck close to the center of the dial. This experience added to Kemal's reputation for indestructibility. After the battle, Liman von Sanders asked for and received the watch as a souvenir. In return, von Sanders gave him an expensive chronometer engraved with the von Sanders coat of arms.

The Allies tried another attack on Tekke Tepe and were again beaten back. Finally, Sir Ian Hamilton realized that they had failed. He thought that the Turks had superior numbers, more reserves, and higher morale than his men. Without the element of surprise, 100,000 additional troups were needed to resume the offensive. He observed: "We are now up against the main Turkish army, which is fighting bravely and is well commanded." By December, all Allied forces were withdrawn from the Gallipoli Peninsula.

The official British historian wrote, "Seldom in history can the exertions of a single divisional commander have exercised ... so profound an influence not only on the course of a battle, but perhaps on the fate of a campaign and even the destiny of a nation."

COURAGE

"We're all afraid of something. Some have more fears than others. The one we must all guard against is the fear of ourselves. Don't let the sensation of fear convince you that you're too weak to have courage. Fear is the opportunity for courage, not the proof of cowardice. No one is born a coward. We were meant to love. And we were meant to have courage for it. So be brave. The rest is easy."

John McCain,*Why Courage Matters*

BIBLIOGRAPHY

INTRODUCTION

Avramenko, Richard. *Courage: The Politics of Life and Limb*.
  Notre Dame, Indiana: University of Notre Dame Press, 2011.

Lappe, Frances Moore, and Jeffrey Perkins. *Y ou Have the Power:
  Choosing Courage in a Culture of Fear*. New York: Penguin, 2004.

McCain, John, with Mark Salter. *Why Courage Matters: The Way to a
  Braver Life*. New York: Random House, 2004.

Tillich, Paul. *The Courage to Be*. New Haven: Yale University Press,
  1952.

CHAPTERS 1 and 2

Ausubel, Nathan, ed. *A Treasury of Jewish Folklore: Stories,
  Traditions, Legends, Humor, Wisdom, and Folk Songs of the
  Jewish People*. New York: Crown, 1948.

Baldwin, James. *Favorite Tales of Long Ago*. New York:
  E. P. Dutton, 1955.

—. *Fifty Famous People: A Book of Short Stories*. New York:
  American Book, 1912.

—. *Fifty Famous Stories Retold*. New York: American Book, 1896.

—. *Thirty More Famous Stories Retold*. New York:
  American Book, 1905.

Barnard, Mary. *The Mythmakers*. Athens, Ohio:
  Ohio University Press, 1966.

Becquer, Gustavo Adolfo. *Romantic Legends of Spain*.
  New York: Thomas Y. Crowell, 1909.

Bennett, William, ed. *The Book of Virtues: A Treasury of
  Great Moral Stories*. New York: Simon & Schuster, 1993.

Bierlein, J. F. *Parallel Myths*. New York: Ballantine Books, 1994.

Calvino, Italo, ed. *Italian Folktales*. New York:
  Harcourt Brace Jovanovich, 1956.

Cavendish, Richard. *Legends of the World*. New York:
  Schocken Books, 1982.

Colum, Padraic. *Orpheus: Myths of the World*. New York:
  Macmillan, 1930.

Crossley-Holland, Kevin, ed. *Folk-Tales of the British Isles*.
  New York: Pantheon Books, 1985.

Cruse, Amy. *The Book of Myths*. New York: Gramercy Books, 1993.

Eliot, Alexander. *The Global Myths: Exploring Primitive, Pagan,
  Sacred, and Scientific Mythologies*. New York: Continuum, 1993.

Esenwein, J. Berg, and Marietta Stockard. *Children's Stories and How to Tell Them*. Springfield, MA: Home Correspondence School, 1919.

Goodrich, Norma Lorre. *Myths of the Hero*. New York: Orion Press, 1958.

Harrell, John, and Mary, eds. *A Storyteller's Treasury*. New York: Harcourt, 1977.

Hodgetts, Edith M. S. *Tales and Legends from the Land of the Tzar*. London: Griffith Farran, 1891.

The Holy Bible. New York: The Douay Bible House, 1945.

Hurlbut, Jesse Lyman. *Hurlbut's Story of the Bible for Young and Old*. New York: Holt, 1957.

Irving, Washington. *The Alhambra: Tales and Sketches of the Moors and Spaniards*. New York: A. L. Burt, 1924.

Jimenez-Landi, Antonio. *The Treasure of the Muleteer and Other Spanish Tales*. Garden City: Doubleday, 1974.

Lee, F. H. *Folk Tales of All Nations*. New York: Tudor Publishing, 1930.

Mabie, Hamilton Wright. *Heroes Every Child Should Know*. New York: Doubleday, Page, 1906.

Rugoff, Milton, ed. *A Harvest of World Folk Tales*. New York: Viking Press, 1949.

Scott, Sir Walter. "History of Scotland." *Tales of a Grandfather*. Boston: Ticknor and Fields, 1861.

Spence, Lewis. *Legends & Romances of Spain*, London: George G. Harrap, 1920.

Tolstoy, Leo. *How Much Land Does a Man Need? and Other Stories*. New York: Penguin Books, 1993.

Tales of Courage and Conflict. Garden City, NY: Hanover House, 1958.

CHAPTER 3
ST. PAUL THE APOSTLE

Armstrong, Karen. *St. Paul: The Apostle We Love to Hate*. New York: Houghton Mifflin, Harcourt, 2015.

Gager, John G. *Reinventing Paul*. New York: Oxford University Press, 2000.

Pollock, John. *The Apostle*. Garden City, NY: Doubleday, 1969.

Wilson, A. N. *Paul: The Mind of the Apostle* New York: W. W.Norton, 1997.

SIR CHRISTOPHER WREN
Gray, Ronald. *Christopher Wren and St. Paul's Cathedral*. Minneapolis: Lerner, 1979.
Lindsey, John. *Wren: His Work and Times*. New York: Philosophical Library, 1952.
Whinney, Margaret. *Christopher Wren*. New York: Praeger, 1971.
Whitaker-Wilson, C. *Sir Christopher Wren: His Life and Times*. New York: Robert M. McBride, 1932.

THOMAS GARRETT
McGowan, James A. *Station Masters on the Underground Railroad: The Life and Letters of Thomas Garrett*. Moylan, Pennsylvania: Whimsie Press, 1977.
Still, William. *The Underground Railroad*. Philadelphia: Porter & Coates, 1872.

BRIGHAM YOUNG
Bringhurst, Newell G. *Brigham Young and the Expanding American Frontier.* Boston: Little, Brown, 1986.
Palmer, Richard F. and Karl D. Butler. *Brigham Young, The New York Years*. Provo, UT: Charles Redd Center for Western Studies at Brigham Young University, 1982.

ROALD AMUNDSEN
Kugelmass, J. Alvin. *Roald Amundsen: A Saga of the Polar Seas*. New York: Julian Messner, 1955.
Vaeth, J. Gordon. *To the Ends of the Earth: The Explorations of Roald Amundsen*. New York: Harper & Row, 1962.

CHAPTER 4
HARRIET TUBMAN
Bentley, Judith. *Harriet Tubman*. New York: Franklin Watts, 1990.
McClard, Megan. *Harriet Tubman: Slavery and the Underground Railroad*. Englewood Cliffs, NJ: Silver Burdett, 1991.

CLARA BARTON.
Hamilton, Leni. *Clara Barton: Founder, American Red Cross*. New York: Chelsea House, 1988.

ELIZABETH BLACKWELL
Chambers, Peggy. *A Doctor Alone: A Biography of Elizabeth Blackwell,*

the First Woman Doctor (1821-1910). London: Abelard Schuman, 1958.

Ross, Ishbel. *Child of Destiny: The Story of the First Woman Doctor.* New York: Harper & Brothers, 1949.

EMMELINE & CHRISTABEL PANKHURST

Barker, Dudley. "Mrs. Emmeline Pankhurst." *Prominent Edwardians.* New York: Antheneum, 1969.

Castle, Barbara. *Sylvia and Christabel Pankhurst. New York: Penguin,* 1987.

Mitchell, David. *The Fighting Pankhursts: A Study in Tenacity* New York: Macmillan, 1967.

Pankhurst, E. Sylvia. *The Life of Emmeline Pankhurst: The Suffragette Struggle for Women's Citizenship.* Boston: Houghton Mifflin, 1936.

ALICE PAUL

Irwin, Inez Hayes. *The Story of Alice Paul and the National Woman's Party.* Fairfax, VA: Denlinger's, 1977.

Lunardini, Christine A. *From Equal Suffrage to Equal Rights: Alice Paul and the National Woman's Party, 1910-1928.* New York: New York University Press, 1986.

CHAPTER 5
ROBERT BRUCE

Baker, Nina Brown. *Robert Bruce: King of Scots.* New York: Vanguard, 1948.

Scott, Sir Walter. "History of Scotland." *Tales of a Grandfather.* Boston: Tichnor and Fields, 1861.

Sutcliff, Rosemary. *Heroes and History.* New York: Putnam's, 1965.

Tranter, Nigel. *Robert the Bruce: The Path of the Hero King.* New York: St. Martin's, 1970.
Robert the Bruce: The Steps to the Empty Throne. London: Hodder and Stoughton, 1969.

JOHN PAUL JONES

Johnson, Gerald White. *The First Captain: The Story of John Paul Jones.* New York: Coward-McCann, 1947.

Morison, Samuel Eliot. *John Paul Jones: A Sailor's Biography.* New York: Time, 1959.

Munro, Donald John. *Commodore John Paul Jones, U.S. Navy: A Biography of Our First Great Naval Hero.* New York: William-Frederick, 1954.

Sperry, Armstrong. *John Paul Jones, Fighting Sailor*. New York: Random House, 1953.

Syme, Ronald. *Captain John Paul Jones: America's Fighting Seaman*. New York: Morrow, 1968.

HORATIO NELSON

Bennett, Geoffrey Martin. *Nelson the Commander*. New York: Scribner's, 1972.

Oman, Carola. *Nelson*. Garden City, NY: Doubleday, 1946.

Southey, Robert. *Life of Nelson*. New York: Dutton, 1813.

Warner, Oliver. *Victory: The Life of Lord Nelson*. Boston: Little, Brown, 1958.

Wilkinson, Clennell. *Nelson*. London: Harrop, 1931.

DUKE OF WELLINGTON

Aldington, Richard. *The Duke: Being an Account of the Life and Achievements of Arthur Wellesley, 1st Duke of Wellington*. New York: Viking, 1943.

Bryant, Arthur. *The Great Duke*. New York: Morrow, 1972.

Cooper, Leonard. *The Age of Wellington: The Life and Times of the Duke of Wellington, 1769-1852*. Boston: Dodd, Mead, 1963.

Longford, Elizabeth. *Wellington: The Years of the Sword*. New York: Harper & Row, 1969.

Ward, Stephen George. *Wellington*. New York: Arco, 1963.

MUSTAFA KEMAL

Brock, Ray. *Ghost on Horseback: The Incredible Atatürk*. Boston: Little, Brown, 1954.

Tachau, Frank. *Kemal Atatürk*. New York: Chelsea House, 1987.

Toynbee, Arnold. "Mustafa Kemal." *Men of Turmoil*. New York: Minton, Balch, 1929.

GENERAL

Allen, John, ed. *100 Great Lives*. New York: Journal of Living Publishing, 1944.

.Hart, Michael A. *The 100: A Ranking of the Most Influential Persons in History*. New York: Hart, 1978.

Tripp, Rhoda Thomas, ed., *The International Thesaurus of Quotations*. New York: Harper & Row, 1970.

Untermeyer, Louis. *Makers of the Modern World*. New York: Simon & Schuster, 1955.